Mosquito or Man the Conquest of the Tropical World

Rubert W Boyce

P. 126

BIBLIOLIFE

MOSQUITO OR MAN?

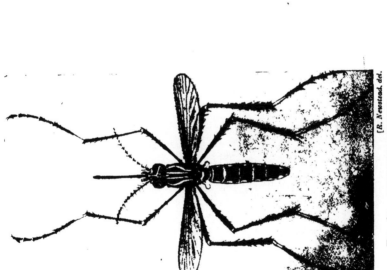

Fig. 1A.—STEGOMYIA CALOPUS LARVA, OR "WIGGLE-WAGGLE."

Adapted from the figure by Goeldi.
Magnified about six times.

[R. Newstead. del.

Fig. 1B.—STEGOMYIA CALOPUS.

Observe the lyre pattern on dorsum and striped legs. This mosquito is the carrier of yellow fever.

Frontispiece]

MOSQUITO OR MAN?

THE CONQUEST OF THE TROPICAL WORLD

BY SIR RUBERT W. BOYCE, M.B., F.R.S.

HOLT PROFESSOR OF PATHOLOGY, UNIVERSITY OF LIVERPOOL; DEAN OF THE LIVERPOOL SCHOOL OF TROPICAL MEDICINE, COMMANDER OF THE ORDER OF LEOPOLD II.; FELLOW OF UNIVERSITY COLLEGE, LONDON; ONE OF THE PUBLIC ANALYSTS FOR THE CITY OF LIVERPOOL

WITH ILLUSTRATIONS

" Stagnation, the great enemy of life "

LONDON

JOHN MURRAY, ALBEMARLE STREET, W.

1909

TO

HER ROYAL HIGHNESS PRINCESS CHRISTIAN OF
SCHLESWIG-HOLSTEIN

HONORARY PRESIDENT OF THE LIVERPOOL SCHOOL OF TROPICAL MEDICINE

WHOSE GRACIOUS SYMPATHY AND ENCOURAGEMENT

HAVE DONE MUCH

TO PROMOTE MEDICAL ORGANISATION

IN THE TROPICS

THIS SMALL WORK IS RESPECTFULLY DEDICATED BY THE AUTHOR

PREFACE

I HAVE purposely selected the title "Mosquito or Man?" or, "Conquest of the Tropical World" for this small volume. I have endeavoured in it to epitomise the Tropical Medical movement, which, initiated in this country by the sympathetic encouragement of the then Secretary of State for the Colonies— Mr. Joseph Chamberlain—and energetically supported by the liberality of Sir Alfred Jones, K.C.M.G., and merchants interested in the health progress of tropical countries, has now spread all over the civilised world. From whatever standpoint the movement is regarded, the reader cannot fail to be impressed with the immense success which has been obtained.

Large numbers of better-equipped medical men have been sent to the tropics, vast quantities of up-to-date literature, dealing with tropical diseases, have been distributed ; the public are being steadily educated to understand that it is by no means an impossible task to make the tropics healthy. In the field of scientific research some of the most important discoveries of the

century have been made—discoveries not only brilliant
in themselves scientifically, but, on account of their
eminently practical bearing, of immense importance to
the prevention of suffering. The movement moreover
has demonstrated time and time again the heroic
devotion of those who embark upon it. Many have
lost their lives and many have been injured. It can
truly be said that no movement of modern times has
called forth such devotion and such enthusiasm.
Finally, if results are looked for, it can be said without
exaggeration that the tropical world is to-day being
steadily and surely conquered. The narration of the
numerous campaigns against the mosquito which I have
here recorded is signal proof of this. The campaigns
show that the three great insect-carried scourges of the
tropics—the greatest enemies that mankind has ever
had to contend with, namely Malaria, Yellow Fever and
Sleeping Sickness—are now fully in hand and giving
way, and with their conquest disappears the awful and
grinding depression which seems to have gripped our
forefathers. Now the situation is full of hope. The
mosquito is no longer a nightmare; it can be got rid of.
The tropical world is unfolding once again to the
pioneers of commerce, who now do not dread the
unseen hand of death as did of old the Spanish Conquistadores of Columbus and Cortes. The British
public has and must always have a paramount interest
in this practical conquest, which is destined to add a

vast slice of the globe, of undreamt-of productiveness, to their dominions and activities, and as a contribution to the history of the conquest this small volume is launched by one who has been privileged to take a humble part in the movement and in not a few of its successful campaigns.

UNIVERSITY OF LIVERPOOL,
July, 1909

CONTENTS

PART I

CHAPTER I

CHAPTER II

CHAPTER III

CHAPTER IV

CHAPTER V

CHAPTER VI

CHAPTER VII

CHAPTER VIII

CHAPTER IX

CHAPTER X

CHAPTER XI

CHAPTER XII

CHAPTER XIII

CHAPTER XIV

PART II

CHAPTER XV

CHAPTER XVI

CHAPTER XVII

CHAPTER XVIII

APPENDIX

LIST OF ILLUSTRATIONS

Mosquito or Man?

CHAPTER I

FOUNDATION OF THE TROPICAL MEDICINE MOVEMENT IN ENGLAND

UNDOUBTEDLY it is to the genius of Pasteur and to his discoveries in Bacteriology and Epidemiology that we must ascribe the foundation of the present investigations in animal Parasitology and their application to the cure and prevention of tropical diseases. The genius of Pasteur lay in its comprehensive grasp, in its faculty of being equally able to direct scientific research to the advantage of both commerce and industry, as well as to the alleviation of suffering. In effect, the great movement which he initiated and the great store of thought which he called into existence in the seventies has proved to be one of the great sources of supply associated for all time with the cause of humanity and the world's progress.

The advent of the experimental method so closely identified with Pasteur and his school pushed traditional medicine to one side and allowed scope for a freer and

1

more comprehensive treatment of disease. This is abundantly proved by the nature and range of the investigations which he himself undertook and stimulated others to take up, and also by the type of investigators which he attracted to Paris. It mattered not whether the disease to be investigated was confined to man or to animals.

He demonstrated that equally brilliant, equally useful and beneficial results would accrue from the study of either. The investigators, drawn from all parts of the world with whom he surrounded himself, displayed the same comprehensive spirit in the treatment of their special lines of research; this is notably seen, for example, in Metchnikoff's handling of the subject of inflammation and infection. Nor were the researches of the great Institute associated with his name only intended for his countrymen, for when he had discovered the cure of Rabies, to Paris repaired the afflicted of all nations in order to be subjected to his treatment. Then there came the period when other countries established similar Institutes of their own, in order that the same spirit of investigation, with the same beneficial results, might be planted in their midst.

Moreover Pasteur had always at hand trained men ready to proceed to investigate on the spot diseases which afflicted tropical countries. His pupils spread far afield, and, fired with the enthusiasm and spirit of their master, they were not slow in reaping a rich harvest in a hitherto almost unknown field of research. Thus, we find Laveran working at Malaria in North Africa; Yersin with Plague in the Far East, followed later by Haffkine in India. Roux and a group of colleagues investigated Cholera in Egypt, and in the present successful movement in the field of animal Parasitology and Epidemiology we can clearly see the direct continuation and amplification of the like comprehensive method of treatment, the same determination to extend the field of medical research and to give the benefits of these researches to less favoured peoples,—just as much to the coloured man as to the white, whether in temperate or tropical zones, and thereby to extend the benefits of civilisation and commercial prosperity.

Just as Louis Pasteur and his disciples, Lord Lister and Koch, gave a new insight into the cause and means of prevention of the infectious diseases, and freed the world in consequence of many of its most devastating scourges, so tropical medicine, in carrying us still further afield, has shown us how to combat other and vastly more devastating classes of disease, such as Malaria, Yellow Fever, Plague, Malta Fever, Sleeping Sickness, and Tropical Anæmia. In these diseases it is now only a question of efficient administration and organisation in order to bring about their total abolition. The result is a triumph of the advancement of medical knowledge, and it is not too much to say that the twentieth century will be known in the annals of medicine by the immense progress which medical science has made into the causes and prevention of tropical diseases, discoveries which show clearly the rôle of insect life in the transmission of disease, and, in consequence, the most effective way of stopping disease.

But not only has the study of tropical diseases conferred an increased benefit upon the science of medicine, it has given new and undreamt-of advantages to commerce, to civilisation, and to administration in tropical countries. To-day we receive regular reports from all parts of the tropical world showing what is being accomplished—the new areas and territories wrested from decay and handed over to civilisation. We are furnished with regular monthly reports from the Panama Canal zone, Cuba, the Philippines, and from a host of other places, just as if they were as old-established as Manchester or Liverpool, and had always known what a medical officer and his elaborate staff were.

But not only has tropical medicine added new territories to civilisation, it has quite recently taken a speculative turn, and, in the light of what is taking place in Africa to-day, surveys what may have occurred in America and in Europe in past ages. Recently Major Ross, Mr. Jones, and Dr. Withington have brought forward evidence to show that Malaria in Greece may have taken no small share in helping to wipe out the old Greek civilisation. What may not have occurred in other countries also? It is even surmised, and not without reason, that the tsetse fly has either cleared the white man out of Africa or kept him out, the fly having proved, until recent times, unconquerable.

Again, in its far-reaching and world-wide investigations, tropical medicine has directed our attention more and more to the rôle which insects play in the transmission of disease, and, naturally, this rôle is not confined to the tropics, our own familiar housefly, flea, bug, etc., being equally dangerous in their spheres. It has also, thanks to our knowledge of the blood in malaria and sleeping sickness, drawn our attention to the striking fact that not every one harbouring parasites shows obvious symptoms of the disease; that there are, in fact, quite as many ambulatory reservoirs, or apparently healthy carriers of these diseases, as there are well-recognisable cases.

I have said that the foundations of tropical medicine were laid upon those upon which Bacteriology itself had been reared, but the commencement of the movement which had for its immediate end the building up of the great subject of Tropical Medicine in our midst, would not perhaps yet have made a start had it not been for the practical and far-seeing Minister who was in 1898 at the head of the Colonial Office, the Right Hon. Joseph Chamberlain.

The following is proof of this, and the history of the movement recorded here is of great interest, because it shows how the layman sees the practical advantage which can be gained by the study of a subject before even those devoting their lives to it can shake off tradition and branch out anew.

Already in October 1897, Sir Patrick Manson in an address to the students assembled in St. George's Hospital, London, had urged the necessity for special education in tropical medicine in the medical schools of this country.

Mr. Chamberlain, in a Report dated May 1903 upon the subject of Tropical Medicine, wrote that—

"It was largely through the interest taken in this matter by Dr. Manson that my attention was more definitely directed to the importance of scientific inquiry into the causes of malaria, and of special education in tropical medicine for the medical officers of the Crown Colonies."

He then went on to state that—

"In pursuance of the second of these two objects it was clearly advisable (a) that a special training school in tropical medicine should be established, where officers, newly appointed to the medical services of the Colonies and Protectorates, might be given systematic instruction with special facilities for clinical study, before leaving England to take up their appointments, and where doctors already in the service might, when on leave, have opportunities of bringing their professional knowledge up to date ; (b) that all the leading medical schools in the United Kingdom should be invited to give greater prominence than hitherto in their schemes of study, to tropical medicine.

"(c) That the medical reports periodically sent from the tropical Colonies and Protectorates should be recast on one uniform type, designed to throw light on the diseases which are prevalent in tropical countries, and to indicate the methods likely to be most successful in preventing or curing such disease."

Previously, on March 11, 1898, Mr. Chamberlain had addressed a circular letter to the General Medical

Council and the leading medical schools of the United Kingdom pointing out—

" The importance of ensuring that all medical officers selected for appointment in the tropics should enter on their careers with the expert knowledge requisite for dealing with such diseases as are prevalent in tropical climates, and that it was very desirable that, before undergoing such special training, the future medical officers of the Colonies should be given facilities in the various medical schools for obtaining some preliminary knowledge of the subject." . . . " I would be prepared," he added, " to give preference, in filling up medical appointments in the Colonies, to those candidates who could show that they had studied this branch of medicine, especially if some certificate or diploma to that effect were forthcoming."

As the result of this letter the General Medical Council replied as follows :

" That, while the Council is not prepared to recommend that tropical medicine should be made an obligatory subject of the medical curriculum, it deems it highly advisable, in the public interest, that arrangements should forthwith be made by the Government for the special instruction in tropical medicine, hygiene, and climatology of duly qualified medical practitioners, who are selected for the Colonial medical service, or who otherwise propose to practise in tropical countries."

Two great ports in Great Britain having medical facilities also replied favourably, and proceeded at once to found schools of tropical medicine.

In the autumn of 1898 the London and Liverpool Schools were founded, so that commendable promptitude was taken in these two cities to give practical effect to Mr. Chamberlain's wishes.

The founder of the Liverpool School was Sir Alfred Jones, K.C.M.G., who then became the first chairman of the school. By thus placing at the head of tropical medicine in Liverpool a great and distinguished business man having large interests in the tropics, the school was at once drawn into close relationship with the mercantile community of Liverpool, especially with that portion more directly interested in the trade of our tropical possessions. The interest in the local movement was, however, not confined to the mercantile community; the late Earl Derby and the Countess of Derby, the Duke of Northumberland, Earl Cromer, and many others took a keen interest in the movement. Expeditions were organised and dispatched to all parts of the tropical world to study the diseases on the spot, a necessity which Mr. Chamberlain had already insisted upon. The gain of this has been, that not only has our knowledge of the diseases been immensely increased, but the way has been pointed out of preventing their spreading or suppressing them altogether.

Both schools entered into friendly rivalry with one another in equipping and sending out investigators, and both at the same time started courses of instruction for medical officers proceeding to the tropics. Nor were the services of the schools confined to British possessions; they were freely consulted by foreign Governments, and, thanks to the fact that Sir Patrick Manson,

K.C.M.G., was the head of the London School, and Major Ross, C.B., the Professor of Tropical Medicine in the Liverpool School, the keenest intellects from all over the world were attracted both to Liverpool and to London for the purpose of study and research.

In the Appendix will be seen the number of expeditions dispatched under the auspices of the Colonial Office, the Royal Society, and the London and Liverpool Schools respectively. Of course these investigations into tropical diseases could not be carried out without very considerable risk. Indeed several of the investigators have sacrificed their lives in this endeavour to advance the cause of medicine and humanity. The Liverpool School of Tropical Medicine has lost two brilliant investigators, Dr. Walter Myers, who died of yellow fever whilst investigating that disease at Para, and Dr. Everett Dutton, who died of relapsing fever in Central Africa whilst investigating sleeping sickness. The London School lost the son of Sir Patrick Manson —a young medical man of great promise who died through accident whilst on an expedition. He had previously submitted himself to be inoculated by infected malaria mosquitos and had contracted the disease, thus proving in his own person conclusively what Ross had previously proved in birds, that the infected Anopheles was the carrier of the parasite of malaria.

Mr. Chamberlain did not rest satisfied with seeing the foundation of these schools, for in a letter to Lord Lister he states: "I am not satisfied to rest at this point, and wish to invite the co-operation of the Royal Society in taking further steps."

He went on to suggest that a thorough investigation should be undertaken by scientific experts on the spot, into "the origin, the transmission, and the possible prevention and remedies of tropical diseases, especially of such deadly forms of sickness as the malarial and blackwater fevers prevalent on the West African Coast," and that the inquirers should be appointed by and take instructions from the Royal Society. The Royal Society immediately appointed a small committee as proposed, and dispatched, in 1898, an expedition to investigate malaria upon the lines of Major Ross's discoveries.

This committee has continued its work, and has embraced the investigation of other tropical diseases (see Appendix). The foundation of the Schools of Tropical Medicine, and the increased importance attached to tropical research by the Royal Society, soon began to react both at home and abroad. Under the guidance of Sir David Bruce many investigations were set on foot in the Army Medical Department, which have resulted in most fruitful work, especially that of Sir Charles Leishman. Abroad, the question of establishing tropical schools was soon taken up, and tropical schools were established at Hamburg, Paris, and Bordeaux.

In the United States also, *pari passu* with this development, increased attention was directed to tropical medicine, and Washington has become the head centre of tropical entomology and parasitology.

Finally, India and the Colonies have realised the necessity of doing something, and great progress has been made in the way of establishing laboratories under the direction of experts for the study of the diseases peculiar to the particular colony. Quite recently a Tropical School has been founded in Australia, under the directorship of Dr. Anton Breinl; splendid work has also been accomplished by the Wellcome Research Laboratories at Khartoum, under Dr. Balfour.

I will in the following pages bring forward the bed-rock facts upon which I base my assertion that in the study of tropical medicine—that is to say, by the study of a wider medicine as distinguished from the parochial, local, or older form—nations possess a force which above all others can wrest vast provinces from the sway of the insect pests which, though minute in size, yet in their aggregate mass have defied and hurled back man when he has ventured into their domain, or completely wiped out those who tried to gain a foothold. The narrative would appear more like a fairy tale were it not based upon easily accessible reports and figures.

CHAPTER II

BEFORE proceeding to describe in detail the fight against the mosquito, I will in the following chapters deal with those factors which prepared the way for the successful anti-mosquito campaign of to-day.

In the first place, I deal in this chapter with the growth of general sanitation. It stands to reason that our tropical possessions have not stood still as regards general sanitary progress. Just as hygiene and sanitation have made great strides in the older countries, and better means of water supply and sewage disposal have been devised, as well as regulations formulated for dealing with the construction of more healthy houses, town planning, slaughter houses, isolation hospitals, milk and food supply, and the numerous other improvements which are naturally grouped under sanitary reforms, so in the tropics steady progress has also been made. There are in many colonies building regulations, excellent isolation and general hospitals, nursing arrangements, slaughter houses, arrangements for scavenging, sewage and night soil disposal, storm

Fig. 2.—A WELL-CONSTRUCTED DRAIN AND STANDPIPE, THE AGENTS WHICH HAVE CAUSED THE DIMINUTION OF MOSQUITOS, TRINIDAD.

p. 12]

water drainage, water supply, etc. The result has been, as in Europe, that many of the tropical towns are vastly more healthy than fifty years ago. By the segregation of infectious diseases there has been a very great saving in life. Cases of leprosy are now housed in excellent lazarettos, and are removed from the possibility of communicating that disease to others; so also with smallpox and other diseases.

The growth and extension of tropical towns has, of course, brought with it the drainage of the soil and the swamp lands which usually existed in the earlier days of colonisation. The necessity for providing for the removal of storm water, and therefore the necessity of making properly macadamised roads, with suitable surfaces and concrete side drains, have freed many towns of the puddles which formerly were the rule in the rainy reason, and which are still to be found in outlying villages or in the small towns of backward colonies where hygiene has made little progress. Therefore, with the improved drainage there has been a progressive diminution of the breeding places of mosquitos, and, in consequence, mosquitos are becoming less numerous in the towns.

Another most important factor which has tended in the same direction has been the introduction of pipe-borne water to the houses and to stand-pipes along the roads. This has naturally brought about the closing of the old-time wells, the common cause of typhoid, dysentery, and cholera in the 'fifties in all tropical towns. One can say that *with the introduction of pipe-borne water cholera has vanished,* and that a great diminution took place in the cases of typhoid and dysentery. But further, with the comfort of a constant water supply either in the house or close at hand by the roadside, the necessity for storing water in cisterns was abolished. In consequence, the storage of rain-water is not now the absolute necessity it was before the introduction of pipe water. It is true that the inhabitants of cities still collect it for washing purposes, but this will disappear in time. Now in the old days it was the storage of rain-water in the wooden vats or in the innumerable barrels which furnished the ideal breeding grounds of the house mosquitos. Therefore to *the new water supplies must be ascribed the remarkable diminution of yellow fever throughout the West Indies*—that is, when we compare to-day with the condition of affairs fifty years ago. But this is a matter to which I will again refer in detail. The significance of the relationship of the diminution of yellow fever to the introduction of pipe-borne water is due entirely to the fact that there has been of necessity a diminution of the common breeding places of the house mosquito—the *Stegomyia calopus*—the sole carrier of yellow fever.

Again, with the inculcation of the principles of cleanliness, and with the appointment of sanitary inspectors to see that yards and gardens are kept clean, there has been a very general cleaning up of the larger towns, so that now there are fewer odd tins and bottles for water to collect in. This, again, has still further reduced the breeding places of domestic mosquitos.

Therefore it is not to be wondered at that in many

Fig. 3.—A WELL-MADE ROAD WITH CONCRETE SIDE-DRAINS, TRINIDAD.

p. 14]

of the larger towns in the tropical and subtropical countries there has been a very real diminution of mosquito-carried diseases. For instance, New Orleans was once notorious for its malaria. Endemic malaria now no longer exists in the town. The malaria-carrying mosquito has been driven further and further out, until to-day he only survives along the fringes of the marsh lands outside the city.

But whilst to general sanitation we must ascribe increased healthiness and a diminution of death and sickness rates and of malaria, nevertheless there is one disease—namely, yellow fever—which persisted, in spite of sanitary reform carried out on the general lines such as are employed in Europe. The town of Rio de Janeiro was an example of this. In spite of the fact that Rio had made immense strides in general sanitation, as disclosed by the annual health returns furnished regularly by the medical officer of health, nevertheless it soon became apparent that there was one disease which did not disappear, in spite of the general hygiene—this disease was yellow fever. It was not until special sanitary measures were specifically directed to it that the disease was stopped. Small-pox has furnished a similar example. By means of isolation and general sanitation and disinfection small-pox can be decreased. But the specific method of attack is vaccination. Then, given this specific method of prophylaxis, coupled with provision for isolation and general sanitary reform, the disease disappears. So with yellow fever, general sanitary reform, coupled with the only direct form of attack known to medical science—namely, the destruction of the yellow fever mosquito,—and yellow fever disappears *in toto*. So that by the term "applied hygiene," I wish the reader to understand the adoption of measures specifically directed to the destruction of those insects or parasites which are directly concerned with spreading infectious diseases, and to bear in mind that the measures necessary against one disease are not necessarily those suitable for other diseases. That, in other words, each disease, like malaria, yellow fever, Malta fever, sleeping sickness, ankylostomiasis, etc., etc., requires the application of its own special prophylactic measures.

In subsequent chapters I will deal in detail with these specific measures, and will be able to show the astonishing improvement in tropical sanitation which has taken place as the result of specially applied hygienic measures, results, moreover, which would in all probability have never been achieved if reliance had been placed solely on general sanitation.

general sanitation plus specially applied hygienic measures for each different disease

FIG. 4.—A LARGE CONCRETE DRAIN TO CARRY OFF STORM WATER, TRINIDAD.

CHAPTER III

MIASM, TRADITION AND PREJUDICE

It is only those who have been practically engaged in anti-malarial and anti-yellow fever prophylaxis who have any idea of the depth to which the old doctrine of the miasmatic origin of these diseases has sunk into the minds of men.

On account of this deep-seated belief in man, the pioneer finds it far more easy to overthrow the strongholds of the disease-carrying mosquito than to overthrow this deep-seated prejudice, which begets apathy and indifference, characteristic of the tropical countries where these diseases are so prevalent. I suppose it is not to be wondered at, considering in the first place the enormous mass of literature which has been written upon the so-called deadly miasm, the veritable nightmare of the tropics, which surrounds you on all sides, which you encounter at its worst in the cool eventide or early morning. It was especially bad over the marsh and in the mangrove swamp, and if any colony was so foolhardy as to engage in dredging the harbour or the river bar or in constructing a new road, or so rash as to disturb an old and disused cemetery, then the wise men of the colony foretold that an epidemic would without fail arise in consequence; of course, in those days it often did, but as we shall see, not from the miasm but from causes now as clearly proven as the law of gravitation.

By the word "miasm" is implied an exhalation or emanation from the soil, especially that of warm, moist climates where there must always be an abundance of decaying vegetable humus. In the name "Malaria," or bad air, given to one of the largest groups of miasmatic diseases, we see clearly what was implied by miasm, and we can also understand why people were so frightened at disturbing the soil. As tropical countries must, owing to the luxuriance of vegetation, have always a vast amount of fermenting vegetable matter, it was clear then that miasm came to be regarded as the necessary evil of tropical countries, and thus it came about that this nightmare theory of disease was accepted as inevitable—it did not matter, every one had to suffer alike from it; they had to get the "*acclimatisation* fever," and then they were "*salted*," and regarded as immune. Malaria and yellow fever were the "diseases of the new-comers"; after an apprenticeship to the tropics they would recover. The miasm was not peculiar to swamps or churchyards or mud-banks; it could equally well be incubated on board ship, from bilge water, ballast, and certain forms of cargo. Learned works were written, in which the kinds of cargo are specified which are most prone to engender deadly miasm.

So bad has this nightmare been at times, that

FIG 5.—A SO-CALLED YELLOW FEVER HOUSE, BARBADOS.

granite sets and gravel ballast have been consigned to the deep, lest an epidemic should break out were they landed. It is almost impossible to realise to-day the incubus which this nightmare has been upon the world's progress. In the old days, the young man, be he soldier, sailor, or young merchant, went to what was known as the " white man's grave." The result was that in many instances only the wilder ones who could not succeed at home went to what was regarded as almost certain death ; and indeed it often was, when one recollects, as shown in the mortality statistics of fifty years ago, that amongst the British garrisons 69 per cent. was not an infrequent mortality rate !

Further, the nightmare even spread to houses and barracks, and men spoke of " yellow fever houses " with bated breath, just as children do of haunted houses. It does seem strange that in this the twentieth century similar superstitions still survive ; nevertheless they do, as those whose duty it is to teach the present-day methods of health preservation only too well know. I reproduce a picture of a so-called yellow fever house. It was supposed that if any one was so foolhardy as to sleep in one, yellow fever was certain to result. No words of mine could describe the loss of life and goods and the curtailment of civilisation which this nightmare of the tropics has brought about.

But is there any foundation for this belief, which has so deeply grafted itself upon mankind ? None whatever. The damp vapour or the small quantity of marsh gas or sulphuretted hydrogen which could come from a tropical marsh is absolutely unable to give diseases like malaria and yellow fever. Could they do so we would naturally expect yellow fever and malaria in colder climes where there are certainly marshes and offensive smells, but where, nevertheless, there is no malaria nor yellow fever.

At the present time the world is seeing the spectacle of the refutation of the miasm nightmare in the Isthmus of Panama. Here there are some 48,000 workmen employed digging the canal in what was formerly a notorious yellow-fever and malarial country. Notwithstanding this and the fact that the graves of the 50,000 workmen who perished of these very diseases in the time of De Lesseps must have been turned up over and over again, no cases of yellow fever have occurred there during the last three years, and malaria has been reduced to a very low figure, so that the total death rate compares favourably with any town in Europe. Surely mankind does not want stronger proof. Yes, certain individuals do. I know of more than one learned medical man, judge, and prosperous merchant who still argue in favour of the nightmare—miasm.

With the knowledge which we possess to-day we can of course understand why the marsh should have been regarded with dread. It is, however, not on account of any miasm, but because disease-carrying mosquitos bred there,—two very different things. Experiments were already made, as we shall see when we deal with the subject of yellow fever, to ascertain by inoculation whether the soil of graves in which patients who had died of yellow fever had been buried was infectious or not. These observations showed that yellow fever could not be communicated in that way.

We are wiser now that we have the true facts before us ; but we must freely confess that the medical men of those days must have been both puzzled and awestruck to find strong men struck down by the fever at the rate of 69 per cent. It was not from want of good food or water, or accommodation. No, they were struck down by some unseen hand, and medicine said that that hand was the miasm. To-day we know it to be the mosquito ; and whereas formerly, acting on the miasm theory, not one life was ever saved, to-day, armed with the new knowledge, we visit the miasmatic countries with the same feeling of security that we do when we pay a visit to the Continent. But did no one in the days gone by stand forth and try to stem the tide of prejudice and tradition ? Were there philosophers who saw something dangerous in the common mosquito ? Yes, there were such, as I will endeavour to show in the next chapter.

CHAPTER IV

IT is the rule that all great movements and discoveries
are heralded in by premonitory signs. In other words,
there are always "John the Baptists" who go before.
It is so with the discovery of mosquito-borne diseases.
In the last chapter I traced the theories that were held
about malaria and yellow fever, how malaria or marsh
fevers and yellow fever were attributed to miasms.
In this chapter I wish to record the opinions of those
who doubted this view, and thereby demonstrated
how far ahead of their time they really were. Viewed
in the light of what we know to-day, they were true
prophets. There appears strong evidence that the
danger of flies and mosquitos was known in very early
times. Thus Sir Henry Blake, in speaking at a banquet
in connection with the Liverpool School of Tropical
Medicine in 1908, mentioned how, when he was
Governor of Ceylon, he had been shown a medical work
written fourteen hundred years ago, in which the
mosquito was stated to be a carrier of disease, and
malaria was described as being transmitted by flies

or mosquitos. It will also be remembered that Herodotus spoke of winged serpents. Beauperthuy argues that this term is very applicable to mosquitos, whose poisonous bite he compares in its effects on the human body to that of the serpent's bite. The use of mechanical protection against mosquitos also appears to be a very ancient practice, the means adopted consisting of either smearing the exposed parts with pungent fats and oils, or more commonly by the use of netting; this is seen in the use of our common word " canopy " ($\kappa\acute{\omega}\nu\omega\psi$ = gnat).

Not until the nineteenth century, however, do we find medical men directing their attention to the mosquito, the common biting insect of the tropics. We read that in 1848 Dr. Nott, of Mobile, Alabama, published a work on yellow fever in which he upholds the mosquito origin of yellow fever, and also surmises that the mosquito of the lowlands may be the origin of malarial fever. But it is Dr. Beauperthuy whom we must regard as the father of the doctrine of insect-borne disease.

" Louis Daniel Beauperthuy, Docteur en Médecine des Facultés de Paris et de Caracas, naturaliste français et micrographe," was born in Guadeloupe in 1803, studied medicine in Paris, and graduated with distinction. He was a medical man with a very strong biological trend, and was devoted to the use of the microscope. In order to study a disease he would follow it up, no matter in what country it broke out. It was thus with yellow fever; wherever an epidemic of it occurred in the West Indian group, he set off to study it on the spot. We thus find him at Cumaná in Venezuela, where a virulent epidemic had broken out. In Cumaná he appears to have been made a health officer by the then Government, and in 1853 we find him contributing a paper to the *Gaceta Oficial de Cumaná*, in which he says :

" To the work I undertook I brought the knowledge gained during fourteen years' microscopic observation of the blood and secretions in every type of fever. These observations were of great service to me in recognising the cause of yellow fever and the fitting methods of combating this terrible malady. With regard to my investigations on the ætiology of yellow fever, I must abstain for the present from making them public. They form a part of a prolonged study, the results of which are facts so novel, and so far removed from all hitherto accepted doctrines, that I ought not to publish them without adducing fuller evidence in support. Moreover, I am sending to the Académie des Sciences de Paris a communication which contains a summary of the observations I have made up to the present, the object of which is to secure the priority of my discoveries concerning the cause of fevers in general.

" The affection known as yellow fever, or black vomit, is due to the same cause as that producing intermittent fever.

" Yellow fever is in no way to be regarded as a contagious disease.

" The disease develops itself under conditions which favour the development of mosquitos.

" The mosquito plunges its proboscis into the skin . . . and introduces a poison which has properties akin to that of snake venom. It softens the red blood corpuscles, causes their rupture . . . and facilitates the mixing of the colouring matter with the serum.

"The agents of this yellow-fever infection are of a considerable number of species, not all being of equally lethal character. The *zancudo bobo* with legs striped with white, may be regarded as more or less the house-haunting kind.

"Remittent, intermittent, and pernicious fevers, just like yellow fever, have as their cause an animal or vegeto-animal virus, the introduction of which into the human body is brought about by inoculation.

"Intermittent fevers are grave in proportion to the prevalence of mosquitos, and disappear or lose much of their severity in places which, by reason of their elevation, have few of these insects.

"The expression 'Winged Snakes' employed by Herodotus is peculiarly applicable to the mosquito, and the result of its bite on the human organism.

"Marshes do not communicate to the atmosphere anything more than humidity, and the small amount of hydrogen they give off does not cause in man the slightest indisposition in equatorial and inter-tropical regions renowned for their unhealthiness. *Nor is it the putrescence of the water that makes it unhealthy, but the presence of mosquitos.*"

Readers will agree that perhaps never in the history of medicine has such a carefully-thought-out prognostication received such remarkable scientific confirmation. Beauperthuy made other communications both to the *Gaceta Oficial de Cumaná* and to the Académie des Sciences.

He studied, amongst other diseases, Leprosy. For

this purpose, acting upon his usual plan of investigation, he removed into British Guiana, and it was whilst engaged upon this study that he died at the Penal Settlement, Mosaruni River, British Guiana.

The inscription on his tomb, for which I am indebted to the courtesy of Professor Harrison of Demerara, reads as follows:

LOUIS DANIEL BEAUPERTHUY,

M.D., OF PARIS,

Born at Guadeloupe,

Died Sept. 3, 1871,

Aged 64 years.

After his death his papers were collected together and published in book form by his brother, Pierre Daniel Beauperthuy, at Bordeaux in the year 1891. I am indebted to Dr. de Vertheuil, of Trinidad, for having placed in my hands a copy of this work. It is written in French.

In my opinion, Beauperthuy wished to publish a treatise on insect-borne diseases. There is little doubt also that he regarded the mosquito or " tipulaire " as the cause of very many diseases. Where he failed in his argument was to account for the *source* of the virus with which the mosquito infected man. He believed that the mosquito introduced some poison into man which it obtained from the decomposing matter on which it fed (*matières pélagiques*), or perhaps from decomposing phosphorescent animal substances, as fish. In support of this he mentions that

M. Magendie demonstrated that a few drops of putrid fish inoculated into animals produce very severe intoxication. Then he says, " N'est-ce pas, en effet, une instillation de poisson en putréfaction que versent ces insectes sous la peau et dans le tissu cellulaire de l'homme ? "

Thus Beauperthuy was clear as to the transmitting agent, but fell into error in supposing that the poison was taken from extraneous decomposing matter, and not from the infected man. In other words, he believed that the poison was telluric, that it did not, · however, come off in the form of a gas or miasm, but was carried and inoculated into man through the instrumentality of a mosquito.

Another investigator of high repute, and also of British Guiana, viz. Surgeon-General Daniel Blair, writes in 1852, in his "Report on the First Eighteen Months of the Fourth Yellow Fever Epidemic of British Guiana," that—

" it would appear from the observation of the present epidemic that though, as is well established, a certain high average temperature is required for the generation and continued existence of the efficient cause of yellow fever, it has not its genesis from any known combination of meteorological elements, and may appear at a time when they are highly favourable to general health and comfort ; that the laws of its diffusion differ from those of gases ; that it is impelled by atmospheric currents, but seems to possess some power of spontaneous motion ; that though intense energy of vegetative power characterised the seasons antecedent to and during the epidemic invasion, *its shifting lines of infec-tion and gyratory movements suggest to the imagination the attributes of insect life.*"

Then in still more recent times we find King[1] in 1882 tabulating the facts in support of the mosquito origin of malarial disease, showing how the word "Miasm" can in all cases be replaced by the word "Mosquito."

Again, later, the name of Dr. Charles Finlay[2] is linked up with the mosquito origin of yellow fever. He did much to direct the recent researches on yellow fever to the Stegomyia as the transmitting agent in that disease.

Working in a totally different direction, in a direction which had already been followed up and was well known to the scientific world, namely, the relationship of the lower animals to man in the transmission of human disease, conclusions were arrived at which demonstrated that it was possible that even a small insect like the mosquito could act as an intermediate host or carrier of disease organisms.

It had already been proved that improperly cooked meat containing the encysted larvæ of the *Trichina spiralis* was capable of producing a very severe disease in man known as *Trichiniasis*. Thanks to the re-searches of Virchow and others this disease, which at one time caused considerable mortality, was finally banished by instituting a proper system of meat inspec-

---

[1] King. "Mosquitoes and Malaria," *The Popular Science Monthly*, New York, 1883.

[2] Finlay, "El mosquito hypoteticamente considerado como agente de transmisión de la fibre amarilla," Havana, 1001.

tion. The main points in connection with trichiniasis are :—

1. The persistence in a living form of the larvæ of the parasite for considerable periods in the flesh of the affected animals, like swine.

2. When such meat is ingested the larvæ are liberated in the intestines and then commence to multiply and migrate, and the disturbance produced in the body of man by their activity gives rise to the symptoms characteristic of trichiniasis, such as fever, etc., etc.

3. The pig infected man, man infected the rat, and the rat infected the pig.

During the same period our knowledge of the other intestinal-worm diseases advanced, and the relationship of the phases of the parasites living in the animal to those living in man was worked out. For example, *Tænia echinococcus* inhabits the dog, the dog infects man through the eggs of the tænia infecting the food of man ; the eggs, when swallowed, develop in man into the scolex or hydatid phase, and there are many more examples.

The next great step was made when the relationship of the guinea worm to man, and to the minute crustacean *Cyclops* was demonstrated by Fedschenko and Leuckart. It was proved that the larvæ of the mature guinea worm upon reaching water were taken up by the cyclops. Now if water containing these infected cyclops was consumed by man, the parasites were liberated in the stomach of man and from thence migrated to the subcutaneous tissues where the adult

stage was passed, and so the cycle repeated itself:
man—cyclops—man.

A further step was made when, about 1883, it was
shown that the intermediate host of the blood parasite
Filaria was the female mosquito, and the suggestion
made that man might become infected through the
bite of that insect. To Sir Patrick Manson we owe
most of our knowledge upon this point. By this time
observers all over the world were beginning to inquire:
How is a disease like malaria carried and spread?
The parasite was known, but how did it enter man? I
need hardly remind the reader of the shelves of books
which have been written containing all kinds of fantastic
theories. They nearly all centred on the deadly miasm
—the malaria or bad pestilential air which, as we have
seen, was supposed to arise, carrying the parasites and
infecting every one coming in contact with the vapour.
There were others, however, as we have seen, who held
that possibly the ubiquitous gnats or mosquitos might
have some share in the transmission: for instance,
observers like Beauperthuy, King, Finlay, etc.

Indeed, with the perfection of our knowledge of
the nature of infectious diseases, it was becoming
clearer every day that the "domestic" insects which
infested and pestered man and animals, such as fleas,
bugs, ticks, gnats, and flies, could act as disseminators
of disease. Already, in the case of red-water in cattle,
observers in the States had demonstrated how that
disease was carried from animal to animal by the tick,
which acted as host and carrier.

However, returning to the diseases of man, it was

left to Major Ross to demonstrate in a most convincing manner that the mosquito was the cause of the spread of malaria. Thus a situation which at one time appeared hopeless is now, on the contrary, full of hope, and the tropics are rapidly becoming possible for Europeans.

Ross showed, as we shall see presently, that when anopheline mosquitos, not all mosquitos, sucked blood from a person suffering from malaria, that the parasites which they sucked up in their meal of blood developed in their stomach, and, after certain developmental stages, reached the salivary glands, from whence they were transmitted to man again.

In other words, the anopheline plays the part of intermediate host, just like the dog does in some forms of tapeworm disease, and the cyclops in the case of the guinea-worm disease. It is most important to recollect this, for it proves that the mosquito is necessary to the complete life-cycle of the malarial parasite, and that the former does not merely mechanically carry the parasite from man to man like the common house-fly does. The latter picks up on its body or mouth parts the infected material, and transfers it on to the first object it alights upon. We can state the case for the mosquito thus:

For the complete life-cycle of the malaria parasite, the special mosquito—the anopheline—is as necessary as man. The date when the parasite was discovered in the blood of man, and how Ross proved that it passed part of its life-cycle in the body of the anopheline, will be set forth in a subsequent chapter.

CHAPTER V

UNDER the term *"Filariasis"* are grouped several diseased states of the body which have received different names, according to their leading features, such, for example, as " Fever and Ague," " Chyluria," " Elephantiasis," " Barbados Leg," " Rose," etc. These morbid conditions are due to the presence of a worm which in its immature or larval form is known as *Microfilaria Bancrofti*, and in its adult form as *Filaria Bancrofti.*

The larval form was first discovered by Demarquay in 1863, and in 1872 Lewis of India found that it was very frequently present in the blood of Indian natives. To Bancroft belongs the credit of having discovered the adult form.

The parasite, and therefore the morbid conditions which it gives rise to, are widely distributed over the globe. It is abundant in China and India, the percentage reaching as high as 50 per cent. in the former country. It is found in the South Sea Islands, and has been observed in the Southern States of the United States, and also in Southern Europe. It is therefore a very widespread condition, and is of very special interest because mosquitos which had previously sucked the blood of persons harbouring the larval forms were found later to contain them in a further state of development, man thus acting as the definitive host and the mosquito as the intermediary host. The discovery of this inter-relationship paved the way, as we shall see, to the discovery of the mode of the transference of the virus of malaria and yellow fever. Therefore, as very great interest attaches to this discovery, I reproduce here the account which its discoverer, Sir Patrick Manson, gave early this year (1909) at a meeting of the Authors' Club. He said:

" Let me go back to my early years of tropical experience. I was then in the island of Formosa. I took a great interest in the diseases of the people. One disease had a special fascination for me—*Elephantiasis*. I puzzled over what might be the cause of this disease, but without finding a satisfactory solution. Later I went to Amoy, a large town on the coast of China, where I saw many more cases and many more forms of the same disease. Still I failed to find an explanation.

" In 1874 I came to London, and there for the first time I heard that Timothy Lewis, who had done so much in the study of tropical diseases, had discovered that in the blood of a proportion of the inhabitants in certain districts of India there was to be found an organism which he called the *Filaria sanguinis hominis*. This is a microscopic animalcule, eel-shaped, and enclosed in a loose sac, or sheath, within which it wriggles about in the blood very actively. It is some-

3

times present in enormous numbers—hundreds in every
drop of blood. These parasites Lewis had found in
more than one instance in association with elephantiasis
or elephantoid diseases. On my return to China in
1876 I endeavoured to ascertain if these parasites
occurred also in China. I discovered that they were
present in some districts in 10 per cent. of the population; in other districts they were present in 50 per
cent.; while in other places they were not found at
all. One thing was certain—that this little organism
was not a mature animal. It showed no evidence of
growth while in the blood, or of any organs such as
would lead one to suppose that it was capable of
reproducing itself. The inference was therefore that
it was the young of some other animal. For this I
searched many times, and at last found such to be the
case, although my discovery had been anticipated by
Bancroft, and by Lewis himself.

"The parental worm was quite a big animal, from
about 3 in. to 4 in. in length, of a thickness of a strand
of fishing-gut. It lay in the lymphatic vessels. But
between this mature animal and its young, actively
wriggling progeny in the blood no intermediate form
could be discovered. The problem naturally suggested
itself—How does this parasite contrive to pass from
one human being to another?

"Now it occurred to me that if it could not pass
by virtue of its own effort from one human body to
another, and if such a passage were necessary, as it
obviously is, some other agent must intervene, and that
that other agent must be one which is capable of
piercing the skin of the human body, and also one
which absorbed the blood of the human body, and
with the blood the little wriggling parasite which it

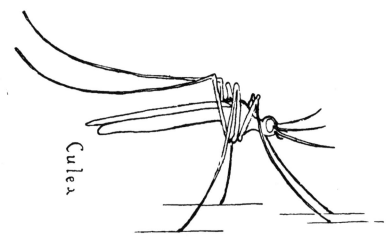

Culex

FIG. 6.—ATTITUDE AT REST (AFTER ROSS)   ONE OF THE
CARRIERS OF FILARIA.

p 34]

contains. Such translation was, in my opinion, a first and necessary step for the parasite to take when it would quit one human body and get into another. Now, the agent which occurred to me as being the most likely to effect the necessary step in the translation of the filaria was the mosquito."

Manson's suspicion that the mosquito was the transmitting agent was soon strengthened by the discovery that the filariæ increased in the blood during the night—this fact he discovered himself after the examination of the blood of 1,000 Chinamen whilst in Amoy. He argued, was this great development of the parasite in the blood during the night in any way an adaptation to the nocturnal habits of the mosquito? Stimulated, as he says, by this further coincidence, he determined to make a practical test—just as, later, Ross did in the case of malaria, and Reed, Carroll, Agramonte and Lazear in the case of yellow fever. For this purpose Manson placed a Chinaman who had the parasites in his blood under a mosquito net with hungry mosquitos. The latter took their usual meal of blood, and then Manson set about dissecting them.

"I shall not easily forget the first mosquito I dissected so charged. I tore off its abdomen, and by rolling a pen-holder from the free end of the abdomen to the severed end, I succeeded in expressing the blood the stomach contained. Placing this under the microscope, I was gratified to find that, so far from killing the filaria, the digestive juices of the mosquito seemed to have stimulated it to fresh activity."

Having thus proved that the filariæ were taken up by the mosquito in its meal of blood and that they were not killed, he next set to work to find out whether they underwent any changes in the body of the mosquito ; this he succeeded in doing.

Manson observed that when the human blood entered the stomach of the mosquito, it became thickened in consequence of the water which it contained becoming absorbed. The filariæ which found themselves imprisoned in the stomach of the mosquito became actively motile. After a series of patient dissections Manson was able to trace them through the stomach wall into the abdominal cavity, and then into the thoracic muscles of the mosquito. More than that, " I ascertained," adds Manson, " that during the passage the little parasite increased enormously in size. From measuring about $\frac{1}{100}$ of an inch in length it grew to about $\frac{1}{16}$ of an inch, and it was now just visible to the naked eye. It developed a mouth, an alimentary canal. Manifestly, it was on the road to a new human host."

When this state of development was reached in the mosquito, Manson supposed that the latter in all probability died, and that the developed filaria escaped into and infected the drinking water. He supposed that the infected drinking water infected man. Later, however, he succeeded in tracing the filaria a further stage in the mosquito. From the thoracic muscles he found that the parasite wandered towards the proboscis of the insect, and could be found in the sheath of that organ, where it remained to await an opportunity to escape. And this was in all probability given it when the mosquito sought a fresh victim to get its meal of blood. During this act it is supposed that the parasite escapes into the tissues of the victim. From these observations it seems highly probable that filaria disease is transmitted from a person in whose blood the parasites are present by the intermediate host, the mosquito, which in its turn infects man when it bites him. Man harbouring the parasite is the reservoir, the mosquito is the carrier. It will be observed that the carrier is the " mosquito "—often a species of *Culex*. But this function does not appear to be limited, as is malaria, to the Anophelines, or, as in yellow fever, to the Stegomyia, probably several species of mosquito being able to act as hosts. But as in the case of malarial parasites, so in the case of the filaria, the parasite passes part of its existence in man and part in the mosquito ; *both man and the mosquito are necessary for the complete development of the parasite.*

Therefore, if the mosquito is destroyed, the life-cycle of the parasite is destroyed and the disease must of necessity cease. This constitutes, as we said in a former chapter, the fundamental principle of prophylaxis in all the mosquito-borne diseases.

CHAPTER VI

THE DISCOVERY OF THE PARASITE OF MALARIA IN THE BLOOD OF MAN BY LAVERAN, AND OF ITS FURTHER DEVELOPMENT AND PASSAGE THROUGH THE MOSQUITO BY ROSS

HAVING in the preceding chapters traced how men's minds were gradually being turned to the possible danger of the mosquito in relationship to disease, and thus in some measure preparing the way to the great discovery of Ross that one particular genus of mosquito could alone communicate malaria from man to man, I will in this chapter refer first to the discovery of the malarial parasite in the blood of man by Laveran and others, and then I will deal fully with the discovery of Ross.

Whilst, as we have already seen in the preceding pages, the marsh fevers or malaria were attributed to emanations or miasms from swamps, investigators following other lines had searched the blood of man by means of the microscope to try to find something in the blood-stream—some organism to which the very characteristic febrile symptoms of malaria might be definitely ascribed. This quest was but natural, and

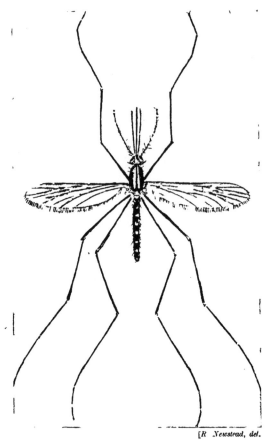

[R. Newstead, del.

FIG. 7 —ANOPHELES MOSQUITO. OBSERVE SPOTTED WINGS.

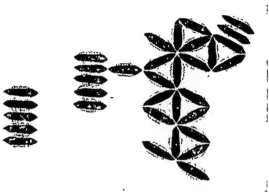

FIG. 8.—RAFTS OF EGGS OF AN ANOPHELINE FLOATING ON WATER

in conformity with the spirit of investigation of the age. It had already, in the hands of the bacteriologists, led to the discovery of the anthrax bacillus as the cause of the disease anthrax, the tubercle bacillus as the cause of tuberculosis, the typhoid bacillus as the cause of typhoid fever, the cholera bacillus as the cause of cholera, etc. Considerations like these no doubt stimulated one of Pasteur's disciples to patiently investigate the blood of patients suffering from malaria, for Laveran succeeded in 1880 in discovering the parasite in the blood of all cases of malaria. His researches were published in his well-known work "La Paludisme," a work based upon extensive observations made in Algeria. After these observations, which were soon confirmed by distinguished observers all over the world, there remained no possible doubt that the only cause of the disease known as malarial fever was a microscopic parasite which multiplied in enormous numbers in the blood of the infected patient. Then, as invariably happens, it was soon proved that related organisms could be found in numerous species of animals; in other words, that this parasite was a widely distributed blood parasite both in the blood of man and animals.

This discovery was an immense advance. The parasite which caused all the characteristic symptoms was now seen, and for the first time described and classified. But whence did it come? How did it get into the blood of men? Did it gain access to the body of man in some finely divided form in miasm or vapours from the marsh? You will recollect that Dr. Beauperthuy imagined that the marsh mosquito absorbed some telluric poison derived from decaying animal or vegetable matter, and in its bite communicated this poison to man. Laveran's discovery showed at once that the virus was not a poison or ptomaine such as would be obtained from decaying matter, but was indeed a comparatively highly organised living body, actively motile, at certain stages in the blood. Then the great question arose in men's minds, how did Laveran's parasite get into the blood? My colleague —Professor Major Ross—answered the question, and we can with truth say that, side by side with the discovery of the bacterial origin of the infective diseases by Pasteur, this will remain one of the epoch-making discoveries in medical science, which will prevent an immense amount of suffering through sickness and death and will advance civilisation and commerce in hitherto almost inaccessible regions in a manner previously undreamt of. The discovery was only made in 1897, and consisted in Ross being able to infect certain mosquitos, the *Anophelinæ*, with the malarial parasite. And then, as if by magic, the true story of malarial infection, about which countless books had been written containing an equal number of hypotheses, theories, warnings, and surmises, was made as clear as daylight. A water-breeding mosquito sucked, not decomposed vegetable or animal matter at the marsh, but the blood of a man suffering from malaria, and in which there were parasites in abundance. The parasites sucked in with the meal of blood underwent further development in the mosquito, *i.e.*

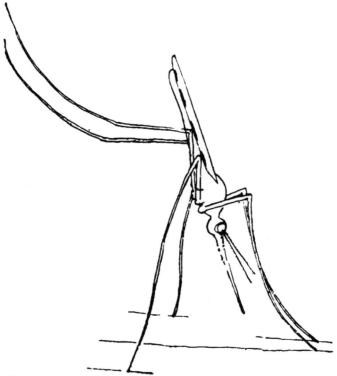

FIG. 9.—CHARACTERISTIC ATTITUDE OF AN ANOPHELINE (AFTER ROSS).
THE MOSQUITO WHICH TRANSMITS MALARIA.

infected the mosquito; and then when the *infected* mosquito, which had now become the *carrier*, bit man, it *infected* him.

As the history of this epoch-making discovery is of great scientific and practical interest, I cannot do better than give it in Professor Ross's own words.

Professor Ross had returned to his regimental duties in India; before setting out, however, he had a conversation with Dr. Manson (now Sir Patrick Manson) on the best method of experiment to test whether, as in the case of the *Filaria Bancrofti* discovered in the mosquito by Manson, a mosquito might likewise act as host to the malarial parasite. Ross says:

" We agreed that the proper course would be to select patients whose blood was rich in gametocytes (the name now given to those forms of the parasite of which some produce motile filaments), and to attempt to trace in the tissues of these insects the development of the said motile filaments which we thought were flagellate spores. In fact it was proposed that I should adopt exactly the procedure employed by Manson in regard to *Filaria Bancrofti*."

After innumerable failures to find anything definite in the bodies of the mosquitos which he examined for the purpose of trying to trace out the further life history of Laveran's parasites in the mosquito, Ross, being now at Secunderabad (1907), says:

" I commenced work by making a careful survey of the various kinds of mosquitos which were to be found in the officers' quarters, in the regimental hospital, and in the numerous little houses of the native soldiers which constituted the barracks, or 'lines,' as they were called. I found, first, the insects with which I was familiar during my previous studies here in 1895, namely, (a) several species of brindled mosquito, and (b) two species of grey mosquito. But at the same time I was astonished at observing that the whole place was overrun by swarms of (c) a small and delicate variety of mosquito which were at once observed to rest with the body-axis at an angle to the wall, and which had spotted wings. In fact they were evidently of the same genus (though not of the same species) as the mosquito which had been previously found in the Sigur Ghat—a genus, or perhaps family, quite distinct from those of the grey and brindled mosquitos with which I had hitherto been working.

" In the spotted-winged mosquito which I now found at Secunderabad I noticed at once the general difference of shape, the peculiar attitude of the insects when at rest, the marks on the wings, and the appearance of the eggs (as seen within the body of the female when dissected); but the larvæ could not be studied until later. The adults were very delicate, pale brown creatures, which by common consent seemed scarcely to bite man, though they were numerous enough to have caused much irritation had they done so. They swarmed in my own quarters, but seldom bit me. They abounded also in the houses of the other officers of the regiment who, with their families, had remained quite free from malarial fever. Consequently I was not disposed to think that they had anything to do with the disease. On the other hand, the grey mosquitos swarmed in the barracks, but were much less numerous in the officers' quarters; (situated some

FIG. 10.—ANOPHELINE BREEDING POOLS, AFTER RAIN, SIERRA LEONE.

FIG. 11.—ANOPHELINE BREEDING POOLS, SIERRA LEONE.

hundreds of yards to leeward of the barracks). Suspicion therefore first attached to the latter variety.

" I determined, however, not to be swayed by such considerations, but to make a most complete and exhaustive test of all the varieties which I could procure—even at the cost of repeating much of my old negative work, during which, laborious as it was, I may have overlooked the object I was in search of. A number of natives were employed to collect larvæ from far and wide round the barracks. These larvæ were kept in separate bottles, and when the adult insects appeared they were released within mosquito nets in which the patients were placed. The insects were applied sometimes during the day in a darkened room, and were sometimes fed at night. After feeding, the gorged insects were collected in small bottles containing a little water, and were kept for several days before being dissected. The procedure was therefore the same as before. But now, in order to ensure at least definite negative results, redoubled care was taken ; almost every cell was examined, even the integument and legs were not neglected ; the evacuations of the insects found in the bottles, and the contents of the intestine, were scrupulously searched ; at the end of the first examination staining reagents were often run through the preparation and it was searched again with care. The work, which was continued from 8 a.m. to 3 or 4 p.m., with a short interval for breakfast, was most exhausting, and so blinding that I could scarcely see afterwards, and the difficulty was increased by the fact that my microscope was almost worn out, the screws being rusted with sweat from my hands and forehead, and my only remaining eye-piece being cracked, while swarms of flies persecuted me at their pleasure as I sat with both hands engaged at the instrument. As the year had been almost rainless (it was the first year of plague and famine) the heat was almost intolerable, and a punkah could not be used for fear of injuring the delicate dissections. Fortunately my invaluable oil-immersion object-glass remained good.

" Towards the middle of August I had exhaustively searched numerous grey mosquitos, and a few brindled ones. The results were absolutely negative ; the insects contained nothing whatever."

He, however, continued dissecting, and finally he says :

" On August 20th I had two remaining insects, both living. Both had been fed on the 16th instant. I had much work to do with other mosquitos, and was not able to attend to these until late in the afternoon, when my sight had become very fatigued. The seventh dappled-winged mosquito was then success-fully dissected. Every cell was searched, and to my intense disappointment nothing whatever was found, until I came to the insect's stomach. Here, however, just as I was about to abandon the examination, I saw a very delicate circular cell, apparently lying amongst the ordinary cells of the organ, and scarcely distinguish-able from them. Almost instinctively I felt that here was something new. On looking further, another and another similar object presented itself. I now focussed the lens carefully on one of these, and found that it contained a few minute granules of some black substance, exactly like the pigment of the parasite of malaria. I counted altogether twelve of these cells in

FIG. 12.—STREET IN BELIZE, SHOWING GRASS-GROWN AND WATER-HOLDING SIDE-DRAIN. ANOPHELINE BREEDING PLACE.
p. 44]

the insect, but was so tired with work, and had been so often disappointed before, that I did not at the moment recognise the value of the observation. After mounting the preparation I went home and slept for nearly an hour. On waking, my first thought was that the problem was solved, and so it was."

Then Ross proceeds to add :

" The mind long engaged with a single problem often acquires a kind of prophetic insight, apparently stronger than reason, which tells the truth, though the actual arguments may look feeble enough when put upon paper. Such an insight is mainly based, I suppose, on a concentration of small probabilities, each of which may have little weight of itself; but in this case, at all events, the insight was there, and spoke the truth."

Up to this point Ross had proved that the parasite of malaria (Laveran's corpuscles), when sucked into the stomach of mosquitos in a meal of blood after the mosquito had bitten a person with malaria, underwent *further development.*

" I had traced," he says, " the development of the pigmented cells up to their maturity and subsequent rupture and discharge of their contents into the body cavity of the grey mosquitos. I could not see at the moment what happened to these contents, yet upon this point depended the vastly important question of the root of infection in malaria. . . ."

" Hitherto my mosquitos had been dissected in water or a weak solution of salt, and I had had no time for methodical staining. A strong salt solution was now used, and the secret was revealed. The contents of the mature pigmented cells did not consist of clear fluid, but of a multitude of delicate, thread-like bodies, which, on the rupture of the parent cell, were poured into the body cavity of the insect. They were evidently spores."

Further on in his narrative he shows how the spores here described enter the salivary gland of the mosquito.

" The exact route of infection of this great disease, which annually slays its millions of human beings, and keeps whole continents in darkness, was revealed.[1] These minute spores enter the salivary gland of the mosquitos, and pass with its poisonous saliva directly into the blood of man. Never in our dreams had we imagined so wonderful a tale as this."

Finally Ross, in order to make a crucial test of the accuracy of his observations, in 1898 infected twenty-two out of twenty-eight healthy sparrows by mosquitos previously fed on diseased sparrows.

In 1900 Manson infected two gentlemen in London by mosquitos brought from Italy. They were infected in Italy by allowing them to suck up a meal of blood from a man suffering from malaria. One of the gentlemen who submitted himself to be bitten in England by these infected mosquitos was Manson's own son. As the result of the bite the latter contracted tertian malaria and the parasites were found in his blood. The first attack was followed by recurrences. This experiment demonstrated that a person could contract malaria in

[1] Ronald Ross, " Researches on Malaria," London, 1905, pp. 32, 33, and 34.

Fig. 13.—Street in Belize, showing grass-grown and water-holding side-drain. Typical breeding place of anophelines.

p. 46]

London where endemic malaria does not exist, provided that he was bitten by *infected mosquitos.* Ross had now therefore worked out the whole story. The mosquito was the carrier of malaria *from man to man.* Malaria had no connection with miasms. The reason why malaria was associated with marshes and water was simply that mosquitos bred there.

With these facts proved, it was clear that in order to prevent malaria, it was necessary to protect man from the infected mosquito and also to wage war against it. Now this latter would have been a stupendous task if it meant that war was to be waged against all mosquitos. Here, however, direct scientific observation proved to Ross that the only species of mosquito which could become infected belonged to a single group, the Anophelinæ. So that the question of extermination only affected that group. In consequence a whole army of researchers were set to work and it was soon demonstrated that the anophelines preferred to breed in small collections of water—those with a natural earth bottom, such as small pools and patches of water of all descriptions, margins of streams and lakes, and odd receptacles coated with humus; therefore the problem of extermination was reduced in magnitude.

The workers in the field of malarial research soon brought to light another very important fact, *i.e.* that, as demonstrated by Christophers and Stephens and Koch, a very large number of people, including children, harboured the parasite of malaria in their blood without showing obvious symptoms of malaria. In other words, that these people acted as the reservoirs of the virus—the comparatively " healthy reservoirs " attracting very little attention by the general absence of symptoms and going about their daily avocations much as usual. The people most infected in this way were the *indigenous* population of the district. Therefore the indigenous population who were reservoirs of disease became the source of infection for the anophelines breeding in the small collections of water close by, and the new-comer arriving in the infected zone very soon found himself struck down by malarial fever as if by magic. Of course he was bitten by the innumerable infected anophelines which had themselves contracted the disease from the almost symptomless but deeply infected native population around.

The extent of the infection amongst the native or indigenous population is very great, viz. 80-90 per cent. In black populations the black are the reservoirs. In Algeria, Sergent has shown that it is the native Arab tribes. With the knowledge of the foregoing facts, the lines of defence are clear.

1. Measures to avoid the reservoirs (man)—Segregation.

2. Measures to avoid the anophelines (choice of locality, screening houses, anti-larval measures).

3. Measures to exterminate the anophelines by :
  (*a*) Use of natural enemies of larvæ.
  (*b*) Use of culicides, oils, etc.
  (*c*) Drainage, etc.
  (*d*) Enforcement of penalties.
  (*e*) Education.

4. Measures to kill the parasite in the blood of infected man (quinisation).

CHAPTER VII

In this chapter I will deal with the practical application of the facts learnt in the preceding pages; in other words, with prophylaxis. I will then proceed to give a short history of what has been accomplished since the great discovery was published.

As stated, the lines of defence and offence against malaria are:

1. Measures to avoid the human reservoirs:
   - (*a*) By means of segregation.
   - (*b*) By screening with nets those suffering from malaria.
2. Measures to avoid the anophelines:
   - (*a*) By choice of suitable locality when possible.
   - (*b*) Screening houses (windows and verandahs).
   - (*c*) Sleeping under mosquito nets.
3. Measures to exterminate the anophelines:
   - (*a*) Use of the natural enemies of mosquitos.
   - (*b*) Use of culicides as oil.
   - (*c*) By drainage and scavenging to get rid of breeding places.
   - (*d*) Enforcement of penalties for harbouring larvæ or keeping stagnant water.
   - (*e*) By educational methods.

Those accustomed to take part in anti-malarial and anti-yellow fever operations are accustomed to hear many objections against doing anything. Some will argue, what is the good of trying to do such an impossible task as exterminating mosquitos ? The people who argue thus are generally those who live in large swampy countries and in countries about or below sea-level, where there is always a great abundance of water and very frequently enormous numbers of mosquitos. The answer to these objectors is that in the first place the war is against one particular group of mosquito, the anophelines, which are, moreover, very selective breeders and not found in the middle of lagoons and rivers but only along the margins. In the second place, that as lagoons, canals, large trenches, rivers, and deep marshes are usually plentifully stocked with fish, larvæ are not present. For example, Barbados is an island which appears to be entirely free from anophelines, yet scattered throughout the island there are numerous ponds ; these are, however, plentifully stocked with minute fish, and so no larvæ can exist.

The very first thing, therefore, to be done in an anti-malarial war is to make an accurate survey under the guidance of an entomologist in order to *accurately* locate the breeding places of the enemy, and thus to avoid dissipating energy by attacking useless places, and by so doing anticipate defeat. A mosquito survey is therefore first made, and it is surprising when this is done how comparatively localised will the breeding-places be found to be. Others will argue that the

nature of their occupation necessarily exposes them
to infection on all sides. The answer to this is the risk
of infection can be greatly diminished by the use of in-
telligence and the carrying out at any rate of some (if it
is not possible to carry out all) of the precautions which
modern discoveries have placed in our hands. If health
is worth preserving, then it is business to diminish risks
or to take no risks at all. This is absolutely feasible,
and has succeeded on innumerable occasions ; just as the
" don't care " policy has meant prolonged sickness or
even death.

1. *Measures to avoid the human reservoirs.*—It
having been incontestably proved that the indigenous
inhabitants of tropical countries nearly all harbour in
their blood the parasites of malaria, and that they
have to a great degree become accustomed or inured
to their presence, so that they can go about their
daily work with little inconvenience, it stands to
reason, given the presence of the anopheles mosquito,
that the new-comer would be running an unnecessary
risk did he not try to avoid living in close quarters
with the infected. The new arrival is in no sense
immunised in the same degree as the indigenous
inhabitant, and by taking risks he puts himself at a
very great disadvantage compared to the native.
Curiously enough, precisely the same argument holds
good with the locally and partially immunised native
himself, for it is well known that the native of one
country who is through long infection more or less
immune to the malaria of his native land, yet readily
succumbs to an invasion of the malarial parasites of

another malarial country, in this respect in no wise differing from the rawest new arrival from Europe.

It were wise, therefore, if Europeans would adopt the plan of living as much as possible away from the reservoirs. It is often argued that this is not a humane procedure, but, from what I have said above, why should the unacclimatised new-comer put himself at a disadvantage by assuming that he is as resistant as the native who has had the malarial parasites in his blood from childhood, and has in consequence acquired a certain degree of immunity?

Persons suffering from malarial fever in the house or hospital should be screened in order to prevent the anopheles from becoming infected and passing the disease on to others.

2. *Measures to avoid the anophelines.*—If in the founding of new towns and residences it is possible to select alternative sites, then let that site be chosen which is furthest from any possible breeding grounds, on soil where the rain-water will not puddle and where the water, either by reason of the nature of the soil or the slopes, disappears rapidly. Very often, however, new-comers have to take the houses built in the old days before attention was paid to mosquitos, houses very often which are infected with mosquitos. Under these circumstances it is very advisable to screen the verandahs and windows with copper-wire gauze. This has now been done with the very greatest comfort in many of the more advanced towns throughout the tropical and subtropical world. With such a protection one can live in security, and surely the

Fig. 14.—WATER-LOGGED ANOPHELINE BREEDING LAND, BELIZE.

gain to health for the inmates is worth the outlay. Under any circumstances it is now recognised in every civilised community that a mosquito net to sleep under is as essential as the bath in the morning. Time was when it was supposed to be effeminate to use a net, and what countless lives and shattered constitutions have resulted in consequence! The net now is as essential to a man or woman as any article of attire.

3. With regard to the measures to exterminate the anophelines, a very large subject is opened up. It is in the first place the measure which strikes at the root of prevention, and it is the procedure, as first pointed out by Ross, that we must all aim at. Get rid of the breeding places of the enemy. And the very first thing to do is to locate them. Here the entomologist is necessary to point out where they are, and it surely is a sign of the progress of tropical sanitation that the services of entomologists are being made use of far more frequently than formerly. The closer study of the life history of the mosquito has indicated to us that man has most powerful allies to help him carry on his war in the form of the natural enemies of mosquitos. All living things have their natural enemies, and mosquitos are no exception. They have their enemies whilst on the wing, such as dragonflies and birds, but they are most vulnerable in the larval stage whilst in water. Here they form the natural food of fish and of certain water insects. It is now, therefore, the rule to stock ornamental ponds, lily-tubs, canals, trenches, etc., with fish—larger fish like the gold fish for the larger collections of water,

little fish, like the useful "millions" of Barbados, for the smaller collections of water. Whilst in Barbados recently I had abundant opportunity of seeing the great utility of fish in killing larvæ.

Immunity of Barbados from Malaria.—A most interesting fact in connection with Barbados is the immunity of the island from malaria. This is due to the fact that the "anopheles" mosquito does not exist in the island [1]; indeed it was the reason why the medical men of the island had at once believed Major Ross's theory of the relationship of malaria to the "anopheles," because they well knew that malaria did not exist in the island and also that the "anopheles" had not been found. This fact has stimulated several observers to ascertain why the "anopheles" mosquito does not breed in Barbados. It led to a discussion, and many interesting facts were brought out,—first of all the complete immunity of Barbados from the "anopheles," whilst the other West Indian islands are plagued with it. Mr. C. Kendrick Gibbons, who has resided for many years in Barbados, propounded the interesting theory that this might be due to the presence in the swamps and ponds of Barbados of a tiny fish which exists in such teeming numbers as to earn the name of "millions," whose staple diet is the larvæ of mosquitos.

The "million," or *Girardinus pœciloides*, belongs to a group of fish known as "top minnows," small carnivorous fish which swim and feed near the surface of the water upon insect life. They are most com-

---

[1] According to local authorities.

monly found in water too shallow for larger fish.
They chiefly feed on the eggs, larvæ and pupæ of
mosquitos. They multiply very rapidly, are oviparous
in captivity; in water tanks, reservoirs, fountains,
and lily-tubs they thrive and multiply, and throughout the island they are largely used for these receptacles
both in town and on estates to reduce the annoyance
from mosquitos. I have examined some sixty receptacles containing " millions," and I can testify to
their absolute use in killing the larvæ of the Stegomyia.
In one house I examined twenty-seven lily-tubs containing millions, and in no instance were larvæ present.
In another case I examined twenty-five barrels
containing aquatic plants, and in no case were larvæ
present; but they were present in a dirty stream in
the vicinity. My experience has been similar with
lily ponds, where I have failed to detect larvæ. These
observations have been fully proved, and the " millions "
shown to be the natural enemy of the mosquito in
Barbados, by a series of experiments undertaken by
Dr. H. A. Ballou, on the staff of the Imperial
Department of Agriculture in Barbados, who, by
keeping these minute fish under observation in the
laboratory, has proved that they eat the eggs, larvæ,
and pupæ of both Culex and Stegomyia. So successful
have these experiments been that the Imperial Department of Agriculture is introducing them into other
mosquito-plagued islands. But Mr. Gibbons's explanation was criticised because, in spite of the fact
of no " anopheles," nevertheless Culex and Stegomyia
were abundant. If the fish theory were correct, then

these mosquitos, they argued, should also have been destroyed.

The explanation is very simple: the breeding places of Culex, Stegomyia, and "Anopheles" are usually quite different. Just as amongst the higher animals some dwell in caves, others burrow in the earth, and others again live in the forest, so with the different species of mosquitos, the Culex prefers dirty gutters and drains, the Stegomyia wooden barrels and small receptacles of all kinds, the Anophelines pools, the margins of marshes, lakes, rivers, ponds, and small receptacles coated with a lining of humus. Fish will not be found in the dirty gutters or in drains, nor yet in the water-barrels and small receptacles. So Culex and Stegomyia under these circumstances are not molested, but the larvæ of the Anophelines are exposed to the fish. That this is the explanation I had a further proof in Barbados; I found that amongst the natives there was a very common practice of keeping one or two small gold fish in the drinking-water barrel. Now, wherever I found this to be the case I never found the Stegomyia larvæ present; where these fish were absent the larvæ were *invariably present*. When I asked the native residents why they kept fish in their drinking-water barrels, they always replied that they had been taught to do so by either their parents or grandparents, and for this reason: if a maliciously inclined neighbour poisoned the water, the gold fish would die, turn up and float on the surface, and they could see at once that the water was poisoned; then they would pour out the contents

FIG. 15.—HOUSE STANDING IN STAGNANT WATER, BELIZE. OBSERVE WATER-BARRELS AND CANOE.

and burn the barrel. It is thus that a very primitive custom has now become of practical value, for we encouraged these humble folk always to keep a fish in their barrel—that is, if it' were necessary for them to have a barrel at all.

In Trinidad I also found in certain of the coolie " ranges " on sugar plantations, that it was a common practice to keep a fish in the drinking-water barrel, but they would not inform me why they did so.

Besides fish, other enemies or auxiliaries have been described. The water boatman, *Notonecta*, has been shown by Branch and Patterson of St. Vincent, amongst others, to suck dry the larvæ of mosquitos. Similarly, it is supposed that the water spider helps also in the work by continually harassing the larvæ when they come to the surface to breathe. A most satisfactory circumstance amongst larvæ is the cannibalistic tendencies of many of them. The observations of Dr. Urich of Trinidad and others demonstrate that the larvæ of *Megarhinus trinidadensis* and *M. superbus* and *Sabethes undosus* are predaceous and feed upon other larvæ. In other words, there appears to be a bitter struggle for existence amongst larvæ when they find themselves at close quarters. All these are observations well worthy of further study, for it is evident that man possesses most powerful allies in the natural enemies of the mosquito which may do much to help him to keep under the mosquito pest.

The common artificial culicide is kerosene oil; a small quantity is poured on the surface of the water to form a film, which then prevents the larvæ from coming to the surface to breathe. It is usual to employ this method for cisterns which are difficult of screening with wire gauze.

The method of larvæ destruction which strikes at the root of the problem is, of course, drainage, *i.e.* getting rid altogether of the water in which the larvæ develop. Drainage is carried out in many ways.

Road drainage.—Roads should be constructed with proper falls, free from puddles, with side drains of concrete or stone, which must be kept scrupulously clean, so that it is impossible for water to stagnate in them.

Streams and rivulets in valleys, gullies, and cuttings should be trained so that the edges are sharp, the simplest way being to concrete them.

River canals and pond banks must be cut sharply, so that there are no small bays where water can rest. Regular flushing of drains should be insisted upon. Yards ought to be constructed with proper falls to the street drain.

There is an immense field for successful antimosquito work in drainage. The guiding principle being to prevent storm water or water from any source remaining stagnant in pools or in any receptacles.

Great attention must be paid to drains to see that they do not sag, also to house gutters for the same reason, also to the *water-holding plants*, like the *Bromeliaceæ* or wild pines. It is not easy at first to appreciate the large water-holding capacity of the wild pine. In the Port of Spain—Trinidad—my attention was drawn to them, for the authorities have adopted the plan of cleaning the trees of these epiphytes. One Saman tree which was cleaned up for this reason yielded twenty-six cartloads of epiphytes. The total weight of these was 3·62 tons. As each plant may hold from ten to twenty ounces of water, the total volume of water represented by 3·62 tons of plants must be very great indeed; the water in this Saman tree was probably equivalent to a good-sized pond, capable of fostering a very large number of larvæ.

Educational propagandism.—As part of any anti-mosquito campaign, the education of public opinion must take a very prominent share. In my experience in the tropics, I can state that the public is being educated to appreciate the danger of mosquitos and other insect pests, and therefore to organise to get rid of them. This state of feeling has been produced by the increased number of public lectures given by medical men and teachers, and by the distribution of pamphlets, and by the press in many cases giving increased prominence to all work on mosquito destruction. Primers on hygiene including antimosquito measures are used in the schools. Pupil teachers, police officers, and those who wish to qualify for sanitary inspectorships are now being trained in mosquito destruction. Further, by means of small handbills and posters, the poorer classes are being trained to fully appreciate the danger of harbouring mosquito larvæ.

But, as is well known, education is very well in its way, but unless it is occasionally backed up by the strong arm of the law, little progress would, in the long run, be made. It is now, at any rate in the West Indian Colonies, becoming the rule to inflict penalties if, after due warning from the Sanitary Inspectors, the people have not got rid of stagnant water, or water in which larvæ are found. The beneficial effect of this salutary punishment is beginning already to tell, and will in time completely change the health conditions of our tropical possessions. It is most satisfactory to record that, in spite of its novelty, the law is not resented ; all classes see the wisdom of the measure.

Quinisation.—By this is understood the systematic taking of quinine in order to destroy or reduce the number of parasites in the blood, and so to modify, ward off or prevent the attack of the disease. It is unquestionably a most wise safeguard. It has been used as an auxiliary preventive with great success in many places, and in British Guiana the Government dispense it at the post offices to the labourers; and it is sought after and does good.

CHAPTER VIII

IN his "Researches on Malaria" Ross very truly remarks that "malarial fever is important not only because of the misery which it inflicts upon mankind, but because of the serious opposition which it has always given to the march of civilisation in the tropics. Unlike many diseases, it is essentially endemic, a local malady, and one which unfortunately haunts more especially the fertile, well-watered, and luxuriant tracts —precisely those which are of the greatest value to man. There it strikes down not only the indigenous barbaric population, but, with still greater certainty, the pioneers of civilisation—the planter, the trader, the missionary, and the soldier. It is therefore the *principal and gigantic ally of Barbarism*. No wild deserts, no savage races, no geographical difficulties have proved so inimical to civilisation as this disease. We may also say that it has withheld an entire continent from humanity —the immense and fertile tracts of Africa ; what we call the Dark Continent should be called the Malarious Continent ; and for centuries the successive waves of civilisation which have flooded and fertilised Europe and America have broken themselves in vain upon its deadly shores."

We cannot obtain accurate figures to give us some indication of the mortality and sickness rate amongst the populations of Africa. We can, however, agree with Ross that Africa is to-day what it is as compared to Europe because of its malaria-bearing mosquito. But we can well imagine that such figures would be gigantic if for a moment we consider what malaria does in India. Here we have available data, and they show that there were 4,919,591 deaths recorded under the word Fever in 1900, the vast bulk of which was no doubt of malarial origin. Taking next the military population, out of a total force of 305,927 in 1900, there were 102,640 cases admitted into hospital suffering from malaria.[1]

Figures like these give the world some idea of the magnitude and importance of antimalarial mosquito warfare; they are figures only exceeded by the mortality which was common in the 'fifties in the West Indies from yellow fever, when the mortality sometimes reached 69 per cent. amongst the soldiers! No wonder, then, that antimosquito work is attracting increased attention all over the world. The method of attack is simple and the victory to be gained is overwhelming, as the following narrative of campaigns abundantly proves.[2]

Historically, the first antimalarial work was under-

---

[1] Ross, "Researches on Malaria," 1905

[2] For further information about the organisation of antimosquito work consult "Mosquito Brigades and How to Organise Them," by Ronald Ross, C.B., F.R.S., 1902.

taken by Ross when in India, and subsequently in Sierra Leone. He organised mosquito brigades to do away with the breeding places of the anophelines, to drain the land, or oil the pools,—not every patch of water, however. The rivers and the lakes and large collections of water were for the most part free from larvæ; these latter were to be found in the small collections of water,—pools by the roadway, pockets of water in unnoticed and waste places, ditches, margins of marshes, etc.

ANTIMALARIAL CAMPAIGNS IN EUROPE

THE CAMPAIGN AGAINST MALARIA IN ITALY

In Italy malaria is a disease of the entire population where the conditions exist for the propagation of the malaria-carriers—the anophelines. In addition to the agricultural population, the great sufferers are railway employees stationed in marshy districts, and in military outposts placed under similar conditions.

In 1905 Grassi proved the efficacy of mechanical protection against the anopheles in one of the most malarial areas near Salerno.

In a letter written in March 1909 to *The Times*, Professor Osler, in testifying to the value of the work of the Italian Society for the Study of Malaria in suppressing that fever, mentions how in 1887 malaria ranked with tuberculosis, pneumonia, and the intestinal disorders of children as one of the great infections, killing in that year 21,033 persons. In 1902 an organised campaign was started, the measures adopted being chiefly systematic screening of the houses and the free distribution of quinine; at the same time, by the spreading of a better system of land cultivation, the breeding area of the anophelines was curtailed. The result, according to Osler, has been that the annual mortality of about 16,000 has been reduced to about 4,000, whilst in the army and amongst the officials there has been a similar diminution as a result of vigorous action.

THE ANTIMALARIAL CAMPAIGN IN GREECE

In May of 1906 Major Ross was asked by a British company owning large tracts of land in Greece to proceed there to advise upon the best means of preventing malaria, which was seriously interfering with the work and prosperity of the company. Ross's visit stimulated the work of the Grecian Antimalarial Society, with the result of forming a co-operation between medical men and officials to undertake strenuous measures against anophelines, such as drainage, screening, etc.—with what success the following statement shows:

Within the last year, 1908, the Liverpool School of Tropical Medicine has been informed by the Grecian League against Malaria that their efforts have had wonderful results in the plain of Marathon, which used to be a hot-bed of fever. In 1906, 90 per cent. of the cases of sickness were due to malaria. In 1907, after the first efforts of the League, the malaria cases fell to 47 per cent. of all cases of sickness. During last summer, however, usually the most intensely malarious season, the sickness due to malaria fell to only 2 per cent. of the total amount of sickness at Marathon.

This triumph is possibly more important to humanity than the results of a twenty-mile foot race, and Major Ross adds: "The best kind of international race is that in which nations compete to benefit humanity." Such a race has been carried on most successfully by the Grecian Antimalarial League in Marathon.

ANTIMALARIAL CAMPAIGNS IN EGYPT

THE ANTIMOSQUITO CAMPAIGN IN ISMAILIA

The town was founded in 1862, and contains 8,000 inhabitants. It is conjectured that malaria was introduced by the Italian workmen who were employed upon the canal construction, and who brought the malaria parasites from Italy with them.

In 1877 malaria fever broke out with great intensity and gained in volume until in 1886 it was computed that every inhabitant suffered from the disease. After many fruitless efforts to get rid of the disease, the Canal Company, having been made aware of the new views of the way in which malaria is carried, invited Major Ross in 1901 to advise upon antimalarial measures.

An anopheles survey was first made, and it was ascertained that larvæ were present in every pool and puddle formed in the cultivated land near the town, in the irrigation and drainage canals, and in deposits of water formed by infiltration from the

5

fresh-water canal. No larvæ were found in the reeds or water-plants along the shore of the canal. The breeding places of the anopheles having been determined, the Canal Company laid down a definite programme of extirpation by improved drainage and flushing of all small waterways; large water basins were dried, smaller ones were filled in with earth or sand, drainage canals were deepened and kept free of reeds and water-plants, and regularly sluiced. The result has been that the larvæ have been driven out of the large area operated upon. To still further complete the work, a house-to-house visitation was made, and house drains and sinks oiled and collections of stagnant water removed. These measures have brought about a remarkable disappearance of mosquitos and flies of all kinds, whilst anopheline larvæ have been exterminated in an area which surrounds the town at a distance of some 1,800 metres from the outlying houses. Since 1905 no case of malaria has been reported in Ismailia.

On February 7, 1904, sixteen months after my colleague Ross's visit, I was invited by the courteous Chairman of the Company, Prince d'Arenberg, to visit the town and see for myself the steps they had taken to form what the Directorate hoped very shortly would become a sanatorium and a healthy inland sea-bathing resort for the Cairenes, out of what was, until two years ago, a mosquito-plagued town and a nest of malaria.

In the old days, previous to the antimalarial measures, the carefully planted town and well-placed hospital did not, however, prevent malaria, and mosquitos infested both the houses and the hospital. Indeed, it was found that mosquitos were more abundant in the European quarter than in the irregular, dirtier native quarters. This is now readily explained by the fact that there were far less breeding places in the Arab quarter, where there were none of the garden drains, water-closets, and fountains abundant in the European town. Dutton, in his "Report of the Malaria Expedition to the Gambia in 1902," has called attention to a similar condition in Bathurst.

Following Ross's directions, in 1901 two antimosquito brigades were formed, one, the "Drains Brigade," composed of five natives and one European in charge, whose duty it was to keep all drains clear. The other, the "Petroleum Brigade," consisting of four natives in charge of a European, was told off to add petroleum to all collections of water which could not be removed at once. In addition to forming these brigades, the Company undertook extensive drain-clearing operations and the filling in of a considerable area of waste marshland with sand.

The Methods of Mosquito Extermination—Work of the "Brigades"

In company with Prince d'Arenberg, Sir John Hardy, Mr. William Johnston of Liverpool, M. Duellenec, the Consulting Engineer, M. Doyen the Estate Manager, and under the special guidance of M. Tillier, chief of the Transport Service and a keen zoologist,

I made a tour of inspection. We first visited some agricultural land plentifully supplied with the irrigating channels characteristic of Egypt. The water in these is supplied from the sweet-water canal, and, as it stands at a higher level, there is considerable fall, circulation can be maintained, and a good head of water can be readily obtained for flushing purposes. Once a week the "Drains Brigade" pays it a visit, cleanses the drains by sending down an extra flood of water, and removes any weeds or accumulations of sand. Constant supervision is necessary to keep the irrigating and drainage channels free from obstruction, as the banks are of sand, and weeds grow rapidly. The least stagnation affords a nidus for the mosquito. The large sweet-water canal does not appear to harbour larvæ, the fish to a great extent preventing this. I particularly inquired whether larvæ were ever observed in the sea-water canal. I did so because I was surprised to find fresh-water grasses and other fresh-water plants growing along the margin of the canal. The riparian growth of the vegetation is naturally encouraged by the Canal Company, as it is a valuable aid in binding together the otherwise shifting sand of the sides of the canal. No larvæ have hitherto been observed amongst the plant growth. We next drove to an opposite part of the town, where the authorities had nearly completed the filling in with sand of a considerable strip of low-lying marshy land. This will in future ensure the prevention of the formation of any pockets of stagnant water.

Mosquito Prevention at Ismailia

We next proceeded to the examination of the system of mosquito-prevention adopted in the town itself, M. Tillier taking his own house and garden as a typical example of the others in the European quarter. Once a week the "Petroleum Brigade" visits the houses and pours a mixture consisting of equal parts of crude and ordinary petroleum into all collections of drains and waste water which do not soak away during the course of the day. Petroleum is poured into the water-closets and into the *puits perdus* or sunken pits, which receive the bathroom and kitchen waste. The garden fountain is emptied, and if any water still remains in it which cannot be removed, petroleum is added; it is refilled after twelve hours. Similarly, the stable drains, washing troughs and all receptacles containing waste water are flushed or emptied or petroleum added. The essence of the procedure being to either empty and cleanse and then renew all water receptacles, or to add petroleum when this cannot be done. But nothing must be overlooked, as it has now been abundantly proved that the mosquito breeds in most unexpected places, and intelligent direction is therefore absolutely necessary ; for this reason, the company have found that it is essential that the brigades have at their head Europeans. The work must not be left to the native alone. Naturally here more especially the co-operation of the householder is all-important; time after time it has been pointed out in the malarial reports of the Liverpool Committee that the cause of mosquitos in the residential house or in the hospital is due to the drinking-water cistern or to some equally simple and preventable source. This, too, may be the case in places where little effort is made by the European, because of the apparent hopelessness of being able to drain some large marsh somewhere in his locality. The power of prevention which lies in the hands of every householder in a mosquito-plagued town cannot be emphasised sufficiently, and it is very gratifying to learn that about this time at Cairo, Lord Cromer and the residents around him commenced amongst themselves a local antimosquito campaign. The willingness of the private individual to assist in the work is a guarantee to the public authority—whether a company or a government —of the earnestness of the movement, and encourages them to undertake their share of the larger work of directing and co-ordinating operations, draining, etc. During our numerous drives through the town we encountered only one example of *Culex*, the species of which we could not identify, and during the night I slept without mosquito curtains. In M. Tillier's words, there are no more mosquitos in Ismailia than are to be met with in Paris. On the other hand, at Port Said, and at the other stations in the vicinity, there is an abundance of mosquito life, and every traveller to Egypt in the winter soon realises this fact.

" Since 1905 we have succeeded," writes Prince d'Arenberg, in a letter written to Major Ross from Ismailia and dated May 1909, "at small expense in

abolishing malaria, and this too without having recourse
to complicated measures, but by adopting measures
so simple that they can be applied in any country. It
is further worthy of note that the improved drainage
has increased the yield of the cultivated areas.

Out of 280 children 15 years old examined for enlarged spleens in 1909, only one showed enlargement !

Antimalarial operations commenced in 1901.

In 1903 there were 214 cases of malaria.
,, 1904 ,, ,, 90 ,, ,, ,,
,, 1905⎫
,, 1906⎪ there were no new cases of malaria and
,, 1907⎪ but 4 recurrent old cases."
,, 1908⎭

These facts also show the great saving in money
which the Canal Company must have experienced
because of less sickness, loss of time, and expenditure
on hospitals and additional labour.

ANTIMOSQUITO WORK AT PORT SAID

In May 1906 Dr. E. H. Ross, brother of
Major Ross,[1] commenced antimosquito and antimalarial
measures ; these were rendered necessary by the mosquito nuisance which existed in Port Said, and to
which I have already referred, also by the occurrence
of endemic malaria, and above all owing to the
example of Ismailia. It was argued that what could be
done in the latter place could also be done at Port
Said. The first mosquito brigade consisted of five
men who made a house-to-house inspection to ferret

[1] "The Prevention of Fever on the Suez Canal," by E. H. Ross
Cairo, 1909.

out all breeding places, that is to say, all collections of stagnant water, and when these were located, to remove them where possible, and if not possible then to oil them. This work was first of all tried over one section of the town in order to demonstrate what could be done ; for as one would expect, there were numerous people who argued, what was the use of doing anything? The results of the test proved so satisfactory that the other districts of the town asked that the antimosquito measures should be extended to them. The total result has been to effect a substantial reduction in the number of mosquitos ; and as the breeding places of the anopheles were also raided, there is every reason to believe that malaria will also be reduced. Naturally it is yet too soon to measure the reduction.

THE ANTIMALARIAL CAMPAIGN IN KHARTOUM

In 1904 Dr. Balfour commenced antimosquito operations in Khartoum and vicinity. He organised antimosquito brigades to examine all breeding places, water receptacles, and pools, and then organised measures for drainage, oiling, etc. As the result of five years' work Khartoum is declared almost mosquito-free, and primary cases of malaria are exceedingly rare.

ANTIMALARIAL CAMPAIGNS IN AFRICA

THE ANTIMALARIAL CAMPAIGNS IN ALGERIA

The Doctors Sergent describe in very interesting detail the methods and results of their plan of campaign against malaria in Algeria.

Distribution of Anophelines

They in the first place show, as Christophers, Stephens, and Koch have shown in West Africa, in the case of the black races, that in Algeria the human carriers of the disease, or the reservoirs, are the Arabs, who harbour the malarial parasites in their blood without showing any pronounced symptoms of malarial fever. From this fact they reason that the danger of infection is in direct relationship to the number of indigenous inhabitants.

With regard to the distribution of the insect carriers—the anophelines—they rightly insist that the larvæ are not found in the lakes or in the rivers; that they are, in fact, strictly confined to the edges. They also lay stress upon the fact that careful cultivation of the land diminishes the breeding places, giving as examples the amelioration of malaria which has followed vine plantation, due entirely to the fact that for the proper cultivation of the vine it is essential that there be no stagnant water. In a subsequent chapter it will be observed that the same improvement has occurred in connection with the tobacco plantations in Sumatra, where the most careful irrigation is necessary to produce the best leaf. In this way the carefully irrigated plantations contrast markedly with the improperly drained areas around, and are free from malaria. This clearance of malaria following on careful irrigation is also seen to a considerable extent in tea, cocoa and coffee plantations; but the reverse has also happened where the irrigation has been less perfect and the water allowed to pool, as has occurred in connection with some banana plantations. In these cases the careless planting of the banana trees has brought about, it is stated, an increase of malaria.

With regard to preventive measures, the authors have cited the prejudice which has to be overcome in the first instance. Much of this, they point out, comes of the fact that the older residents cannot understand that it is one special group of mosquitos— the anophelines—which are the carriers of the disease. They are bitten by harmless mosquitos and wonder why they do not get malaria, and reason in consequence that they are either proof against malaria or that mosquitos are not the transmitters of the disease. Or they travel and stay in intensely malarial places, but owing to the fact that they are to a considerable degree immune to the irritating action of the bites of mosquitos generally, they don't feel the bites of the anophelines which are present; they become infected with malaria, but affirm that they were not bitten.

Segregation.—The authors also discuss the marked difficulties of segregation, the colonists being obliged to live close to their workmen. On the other hand, they point out how rational and justifiable it is to protect the susceptible new-comer from the danger of close dwelling with those who, although harbouring the parasites, are not inconvenienced by the disease, but nevertheless are capable of communicating the disease, a disease which will have a disastrous effect upon the new-comer.

Quinisation.—Systematic treatment with quinine of infants and adults has had a very beneficial effect.

MEASURES DIRECTED AGAINST THE MOSQUITO CARRIERS

1. *Antilarval measures.*—These consist in improved drainage: deepening shallow drains and making the margins sharp-cut, and removing weeds ; also oiling.

2. *Measures against the adult mosquito carriers.*— The systematic use of mosquito nets, and the screening of houses.

To sum up.   The Algerian antimalarial campaigns were commenced in 1902, and consisted in :

1. Spreading the knowledge of the way in which malaria was propagated.

2. Giving a practical demonstration upon a suitable scale of the markedly beneficial effects of antimosquito measures in reducing malarial fever, for this purpose choosing a place in a particularly malarial district and subjecting it to the well-recognised antimosquito treatment, viz. oiling and drainage and enforcing nets and screening, and treating the dwellers in the area chosen systematically with quinine.   The result of these measures has been the almost total disappearance of anophelines in the treated area as compared with the untreated district around, and the very marked diminution of cases of malaria amongst the Europeans employed in the selected area as compared with those living in the non-treated areas.   Thus, in one experiment, no case of malaria was reported amongst the seventy-one European inhabitants, whilst twenty-seven Europeans outside the area contracted the disease.

Again, in 1906, of sixty-two Europeans residing in seven stations where antimosquito measures were enforced, four cases of malaria were reported as against thirty-five cases in 1904, when no precautions were taken.

THE ANTIMALARIAL CAMPAIGNS IN WEST AFRICA

The first campaign was started in Sierra Leone; indeed, it was the first expedition[1] sent out by the Liverpool School of Tropical Medicine to put to a *practical test*, as suggested by Ross himself, the discoveries which he had made during the years 1895–1898, as we have already seen in the preceding chapters. This was the first occasion on which a free hand was given to Ross to test the results of doing away with the breeding places of the anophelines. Sierra Leone was selected because of its unsavoury reputation for being the " white man's grave," and also for the fact that it presented great natural difficulties in carrying out antimosquito war; these difficulties were the very heavy rainfall and the nature of the soil. The expedition, which consisted of Major Ross and Dr. Logan Taylor, arrived in Freetown in July 1901, and Major Ross directed operations against all kinds of mosquitos. Thirty-two men were engaged under the direction of headmen, and they were furnished with carts and utensils. The force was divided into two gangs: one a Culex gang, composed of six men, to collect all broken bottles, tins, and odd receptacles of all kinds from the

---

[1] Previous expeditions had been sent out to confirm the accuracy of Major Ross's observations (see Appendix).

FIG. 16.—ROAD POOLS, VILLAGE, WEST AFRICA.   BREEDING PLACES OF ANOPHELINES,

FIG. 17.—ANOPHELINE BREEDING POOLS, SIERRA LEONE.

compounds; secondly, an anopheles gang, to drain pools and depressions in back yards and streets. The members of the gangs instructed the householders upon the danger of harbouring larvæ. The drains were kept brushed out. The result of the cleaning up and drainage was an observable diminution in the number of mosquitos.

Dr. Logan Taylor, as the result of a second and independent visit, drew up a report upon the sanitary condition of Cape Coast Town.

The late Dr. Dutton in 1902 visited the Gambia, and reported upon its antimosquito measures.

Lieut.-Col. Giles was also sent out by the Liverpool School, and reported upon antimalarial measures in Sekondi, the Goldfields, and Kumassi, and there have been many more expeditions of a similar nature (see Appendix).

In 1904 I also visited, in conjunction with Drs. Evans and Clarke,[1] Freetown, Bathurst, and Conakry in the French Guinea, and reported upon the sanitation and antimalarial measures then in force. We found that the inhabitants had commenced to put into practice the teachings of the previous expeditions, and that they realised it was possible to protect themselves from the anophelines by adopting the precautions taught by Ross. We found that mosquito nets were more generally used, the water cisterns screened, and the drains better looked after. In other words, there was a distinct improvement over the condition reported by

"Report of the Sanitation and Antimalarial Measures in Practice in Bathurst, Conakry, and Freetown," February 1905.

previous expeditions. This improving state of affairs has been kept up all along the West Coast. I have just received (June 1909) the following communication from Mr. H. Cottrell, the Chairman of the African Association, upon the present state of malaria amongst the employees of the Association.

In 1904, out of 96 employees 2 died and 5 were invalided. In 1905, out of 91 employees 1 died and 3 were invalided. In 1906, out of 94 employees 1 died and 5 were invalided. In 1907, out of 98 employees 1 died and 9 were invalided. In 1908, out of 98 there were no deaths and 4 were invalided. The employees carry on their work in 35 different places over the Gold Coast and Southern Nigeria. Mr. Cottrell adds:

" You will no doubt find in these figures satisfaction with the result of the efforts of the School of Tropical Medicine in improving the conditions of life in West Africa, particularly so when I tell you that out of the 5 deaths recorded over the 5 years given, 3 of such deaths were not due to the climate."

The Secretary of the Liverpool School of Tropical Medicine has this month (July) received the following letter from the Secretary of the African Association :

" I beg to hand you herewith cheque for £50, being a supplementary Grant made to your School by the Shareholders of this Company at their meeting on the 1st inst., in recognition of the fact that 1908 was the first year in the history of the Company in which there had not been a death in the whole of our Coast Staff."

FIG. 18.—ROADSIDE DITCH CONTAINING STAGNANT WATER, BREEDING ANOPHELINES.
WEST AFRICA.

FIG. 19.—ROAD POOLS, WEST AFRICA.

In reply to special inquiries made by Sir Alfred Jones, Chairman of the Liverpool School, the manager of important gold mines on the Gold Coast states that, during the five years which he has spent in that Colony, there has been a marked improvement in' the health of European residents. This he attributes largely to the work of the Liverpool School in stamping out mosquitos and encouraging better sanitation, but it is also due in great measure to the sending out of a better and more temperate class of men.

Surely the result of the West African campaigns has been a net gain of life and money.

Further eloquent testimony as to the practical result of this African campaign has been given by Dr. Johnston, who has thirty years' experience in Jamaica, who purposely visited our school to bear testimony to the value of our teaching in the prevention of malaria. He himself had first thought that the prevention of malaria by the destruction of the mosquito, as taught by our school, would be a hopeless task; but a very large and practical experience, chiefly amongst the natives, had overwhelmingly convinced him of the practicability and efficacy of the measures put forward by Ross and his school. In his own experience, it has reduced the mortality amongst the native soldiers of the West Indian Regiments serving on the West Coast of Africa some 75 per cent. The preventive measures were not only of use to white trading officials and officers, but also of immense advantage to the natives themselves.

CAMPAIGN ON THE ISTHMIAN CANAL ZONE

PANAMA

Panama, like Havana, has now become an object-lesson in prophylaxis to the rest of the world. Until recently the mosquito absolutely foiled the attempts of man to construct the canal. The French tried it, with a loss which has been estimated at 50,000 men. Anopheles and Stegomyia were more than a match for man. But thanks to researches in tropical medicine, their breeding grounds were disclosed and their slaughter commenced, and regular monthly reports tell us with what marvellous success. Both Sir Frederick Treves and Sir Harry Johnston have already made it the text of very inspiring addresses.

In 1904 the United States took over the administration of the Canal Zone and appointed a commission, and they set to work in grim earnest. A chief sanitary officer was appointed, with a splendid staff of 2,000 men under him.

The following figures show the great decrease in the malarial death rate since 1906 :

Year				Deaths
1906	.		.	. 821
1907	.	.	.	. 424
1908	.	.	.	. 282

or 1·34 per thousand

That is, the death rate from malaria in the Canal Zone, in spite of the enormous increase in the labourers, is only one-third of the death rate three years ago.

This great antimalarial work has been accomplished chiefly by drainage and trimming the margins of all lakes and swamps of all weeds amongst which the larvæ shelter. Superficial ditches are concreted, deep ones are kept free of weeds. No animals are allowed near the margins of the ditches or marshes, so as to avoid making the small foot puddles which cattle invariably make. Where possible sulphate of copper, crude petroleum, and other culicides are also employed. Bush-cutting is regarded as second only in importance to drainage, and with this I thoroughly agree. To enforce and carry out these antimalarial measures in the forty-five miles' strip along the line of the canal, the strip has been divided into seven districts. Each district is in charge of an inspector, whilst a chief inspector is over all. The chief has on his staff a man acquainted with the life-history of the mosquito, another who is an expert in tilling and drainage, also a general inspector ; these men keep in touch with the district inspectors, and act as teachers. Each district inspector has a gang of twenty-five to thirty men, who trench and cut bush, also carpenters for looking after screening ; lastly two quinine dispensers. The medical officer of each district reports monthly all cases of malaria to the central office, and if the number of cases go up in a district there is an immediate inquiry to know why.

THE ANTIMALARIAL CAMPAIGN IN COLON

Colon is a town of 15,000 inhabitants, built on an island just above sea-level, and many of the houses,

6

as in similar low-lying countries, viz. Honduras and British Guiana, are built upon piles, and in the wet season swamps abound, and of course innumerable mosquitos. The bush was first cut away for half a mile to the back of the town; the cleared swampy area was then canalised and small superficial drains led into the larger channels; with the fall of the tide the fresh water runs out, and the incoming tide brings in sea water. I recommended precisely the same system in British Honduras. All barrels and cisterns were rigorously inspected. Result—Colon is to-day almost free from every kind of mosquito. In addition, however, the houses of employees are screened with wire gauze; mosquito nets are used, although the necessity for these precautions has practically ceased; quinine is also taken.

ANTIMOSQUITO CAMPAIGN IN RIO DE JANEIRO

The City of Rio de Janeiro furnishes us with regular monthly returns which disclose a marvellous improvement in mosquito-carried diseases, such as yellow fever and malaria. The city has undergone a complete transformation in this respect.

Similarly favourable reports come from HAVANA and from many other towns in South America.

In BRITISH HONDURAS the antimosquito war, which I commenced in 1905, more particularly directed against the stegomyia, has had its effect in reducing the numbers of mosquitos of all kinds and directing attention to protecting against the anophelines. In the survey which I then made of Belize I pointed out the breeding grounds of anophelines, and how by improved street and road drainage, and by levelling up the submerged compounds, by canalisation, and by removal of all odd receptacles, and the rigid screening of all water cisterns, it would be possible to banish yellow fever and greatly diminish or banish malaria. The result of putting into practice these measures has been a marked improvement in mosquito-borne diseases.

ANTIMALARIAL CAMPAIGNS IN THE WEST INDIES

We have already, in the chapter upon General Sanitation, seen the progress which the West Indies have made in reducing mosquito-borne diseases, brought about, as it was there shown, by pipe-borne water supplies, drainage, and building extension. In this place I wish to draw attention, however, to the specific means which have been set on foot to substantially reduce malaria throughout the group. For it is a fact that malaria is still the cause of a very large proportion of sickness in the islands. In those islands in which there is a well-equipped official medical organisation much has been done. The medical officers are as alive as any one to the importance of destroying the breeding grounds of the anophelines, and it has been in this connection that the entomologists have rendered great service by indicating the breeding places. The use of the mosquito net is very general ; a few houses are wire-netted, and in BRITISH GUIANA quinine is on sale at the post offices. The Surgeon-General of that

Colony writes me as follows concerning the sale of quinine :

"As one result of the Mortality Commission, arrangements have been made for the sale of quinine at the district post offices, so as to place it within reach of the poorer classes. The drug is retailed at the rate of two cents for thirty grains, and meets with a ready sale. It is only intended for the benefit of the people ; and in order to prevent, as far as possible, its purchase and subsequent resale at a profit, the quantity which can be sold to any one person at a time has been limited to 180 grains. Later on, as a further precaution, the supplies for this purpose were ordered in tablets coloured pink and stamped with the letters B.G." [1]

Regulations have also been passed making it compulsory on district boards to properly drain the roads in their respective districts.

Regulations have been passed making it compulsory to screen all water-vats. Lectures are given and health primers used in the schools ; circulars and diagrams are distributed to householders, police stations and public places, drawing attention to the prevention of malaria by the destruction of mosquitos. Similar measures have been taken in Trinidad.

ST. LUCIA

As further evidence of the thoroughness of the movement in the West Indies, I reproduce here a circular letter which the Administrator of St. Lucia,

[1] For Regulations see Appendix.

then Mr. Cork, issued in 1905 to the medical officers throughout the island :

" Being desirous of obtaining reliable information as to the prevalence of mosquito-borne diseases in this Colony, I shall feel very much obliged if you will be so good as to favour me with a return showing the number and description of such diseases which may come under your notice, either in your public capacity or in your private practice during the past twelve months. If convenient to you to add particulars of any other preventable disease which may be prevalent I shall be much obliged."

This letter had a very salutary effect. It showed that the administration was fully alive to the importance of antimosquito measures; it also showed, by the replies received, to what extent the medical officers had kept in touch with modern developments in epidemiology and mosquito-borne diseases; and thirdly it demonstrated where weak spots existed in sanitary administration in St. Lucia, in respect of these important diseases, and where in consequence the medical machinery required augmentation.

ANTIGUA

In the year 1904 active antimosquito measures were adopted in the Colony of Antigua—on a small scale, it is true, but nevertheless something. The first brigade was formed under the chairmanship of Sir Courtney Knowles, who was subsequently succeeded by Sir B. Sweet Escott. The first executive officer was Oliver Nugent, magistrate of Antigua. The brigade work was chiefly directed against the anopheles ; the oiling of all pools was undertaken, and the people were warned of the danger of keeping stagnant water, and crab holes were filled up. To this enterprise the public subscribed at the rate of one shilling each, and the Government gave a small subsidy. The work of the brigade has now been taken over by the City Board of the town of St. John's. Small as was this movement, it was a step in the right direction and ought to be followed by other colonies.

ANTIMALARIAL WORK IN JAMAICA

In a recent (1908–9) malarial survey of Jamaica,[1] undertaken by Dr. Prout, C.M.G., on behalf of the Liverpool School of Tropical Medicine, it is stated that although something has been accomplished in the shape of antimosquito measures, yet the work done is not equal to that accomplished in other places. Prout calculates the death rate from malaria in the period of ten years 1898–1907 to have been 4·4 per cent. He states, moreover, that the deaths due to malaria in 1907 were 4,094, and the total deaths from that disease in ten years 34,695. According to this authority one-fifth of the total death rate in the island is due to malaria. This of course should not be, considering that malaria can be so comparatively easily grappled with. In analysing the hospital returns, Prout states that one-half of the cases admitted into hospital are malarial, and he estimates the actual

[1] Twenty-first Expedition of the Liverpool School of Tropical Medicine, Malaria, Jamaica, 1908–9.

cost of these cases to the Colony at £6,300. Amongst the coolies he states that 50 per cent. of the illness is also due to malaria, which he estimates is equivalent to a loss of 16·9 days out of the 100 working days of each Coolie labourer.

To remedy this state of affairs Dr. Prout proposes to make it a punishable offence to harbour larvæ on premises (this is now the case, as we shall see, in many of the West Indian islands); that all wells, tanks, and barrels should be screened ; that all gutters in towns should be cemented, as is the case in Trinidad; that all margins of rivers be kept free of grass and weeds ; that drainage operations should be undertaken bit by bit but systematically ; that mosquito nets should be invariably employed and houses screened where desirable. He also recommends the daily use of quinine by those exposed to infection, and the application of kerosene oil to all breeding places which cannot be drained. '

The report also emphasises the importance to the Colony of the services of an entomologist. In Jamaica, as in some of the other colonies where there is no official entomologist, a doctor or clergyman or other enthusiast has volunteered his services, to the great good, as I can testify, of the Colony.

ANTIMOSQUITO WORK, NASSAU, BAHAMAS

Measures were started in 1905 by, the Board of Health. Regulations dealing with stagnant water were passed (see Appendix). Quinine was distributed and screening enforced.

THE ANTIMALARIAL MEASURES IN MAURITIUS

In 1907 Major Ross was sent, at the instance of the Colonial Office, to Mauritius to report upon measures for the prevention of malaria. The report is a very complete one, dealing very fully with the history of malaria, and then with the distribution of malaria in Mauritius, and finally with his recommendations for the prevention of the spread of the disease. These include the formation of mosquito brigades, the appointment of a malarial authority, drainage operations, screening, quinisation ; also a measure to make it a punishable offence to harbour mosquito and other larvæ on premises. For the guidance of other colonies I reproduce it in the Appendix with the other anti-larval measures.

SANITARY AND ANTIMOSQUITO MEASURES IN THE PHILIPPINES

The loss of Spain's tropical possessions is partly attributable to her failure to cope successfully with disease. Ignorance of the laws of health destroyed the health and lives of 100,000 Spanish soldiers in Cuba in three years. Complete change took place under American administration (1903), and the death rate amongst the troops in Cuba and Porto Rico was reduced to 6·72 per thousand, or practically the same as at home.

In July 1901 military government in the Philippines was formally instituted. The officers responsible for the health administration were in the first instance men recruited from the Army Medical Service,. and later, in 1905, men of the United States Marine Hospital Service were employed ; all, therefore, were especially conversant with this class of work.

The result of general sanitary prophylaxis is seen by comparing the death rate amongst the troops in the year 1906 with that obtaining in 1899.

In 1899 the death rate from malaria was   1·23

    and the admissions   .   .   .   .   705·49

In 1906 the death rate was .   .   .   0·55

    and the admissions   .   .   .   .   304·20

With regard to the health of the civil population of the Philippines, the death rate in Manilla has been reduced from 40·99 per mille to 30 or below in 1908; figures which compare well with the rest of the world.

(From a paper by Dr. Washburn upon "Health Conditions in the Philippines," September 1908, *Philippine Journal of Science.*)

THE ANTIMALARIAL CAMPAIGN IN RIO AND OTHER PARTS OF BRAZIL, 1903

Just as a most vigorous policy of extermination has been adopted against yellow fever, and with results that the Republic is justly proud of, so, stimulated by this success, a vigorous war has been declared against the anophelines. Rio has always had a bad reputation as regards malaria, but not so bad as usually depicted.

In 1900 there were 1,019 deaths

   „   1901   „   „   932   „

   „   1902   „   „   1,217   „

In 1903 war on the anophelines was declared, and there was an immediate fall to 772 deaths.

In 1904 there were 433 deaths
,, 1905 ,, ,, 295 ,,
,, 1906 ,, ,, 266 ,,
,, 1907 ,, ,, 239 ,, .

Encouraging enough results for a comparatively small outlay—and from all parts of the civilised world where antimalarial measures are adopted, similar results are recorded.

ANTIMALARIAL CAMPAIGNS IN THE EAST INDIES

ANTIMALARIAL CAMPAIGN IN KLANG AND PORT SWETTENHAM

Taking Travers and Watson's figures for Port Swettenham and Klang in the Federated Malay States, we find that at Port Swettenham the area to be dealt with was about 110 acres, low-lying and swampy. In 1901 draining and filling-in operations were undertaken.

In Klang, the area affected covered 332 acres, swampy and bush: drainage and clearing effected.

Results in Klang and Port Swettenham: Deaths due to malaria in 1901, 368; in 1905, 45. In surrounding districts where no measures were taken the corresponding figures are 266 deaths in 1901 and 351 in 1905.

In 1901 Government employees at both places numbered 176, and the number of days' leave granted for malarial sickness totalled 1,026. In 1904 the employees numbered 281, and the number of days' leave was 71, and in 1905, 30.   Surely a considerable saving in money, not to mention lives and broken constitutions.

ANTIMALARIAL CAMPAIGN IN HONG KONG

What do we learn from Hong Kong?—Population, 377,850 ; white, 10,835 — heavy rainfall, numerous breeding places of anophelines.   Operations commenced by Dr. Thomson in 1901 ; works carried out, efficient training and drainage, netting, oiling, and quinine.

Results : In 1901 admissions in the two principal hospitals for malaria were 1,294, and deaths 132.   In 1905 admissions 419, deaths 54.   Amongst the police, in 1901, 44 per cent. ; in 1905, 12½ per cent.   Total deaths in Colony in 1901, 574 ; in 1905, 285.

ANTIMALARIAL MEASURES IN THE UNITED STATES

Dr. A. Woldert, in a small pamphlet entitled " Malarial Fever and its Expense to the People of Texas," has calculated from an examination of various official records that the loss in money caused by malarial sickness upon three railway systems amounted to 133,810 dollars a year ; and calculating upon the same basis, viz. that one person in twelve is affected with malaria in Texas, he reckons the total loss to the State as 5,333,320 dollars a year.   He gives these figures to support the necessity for a vigorous anti-malarial campaign.

Dr. A. H. Doty of New York has rendered excellent service by directing attention to the extermination of the mosquito on the Atlantic side of America, where already much has been done by the American Mosquito Extermination Society of New York.

CHAPTER IX

NOTES ON THE RELATIONSHIP OF PLANTATIONS AND
BOTANIC GARDENS TO THE MOSQUITO QUESTION

MANY interesting facts in connection with malaria have
been brought to light by observations conducted by
medical officers charged with the supervision of the
health of labourers employed upon large estates.

Tobacco Plantations.—Dr. Kuenen, on a visit to
Liverpool in 1909, told us how in his district malaria
had been reduced by drainage. Dr. Kuenen, who is
Director of Pathology at Medan, Sumatra, has the
medical care of the workers upon a large tobacco
estate. The whole of the coast of Sumatra is notorious
for its bad forms of malaria. When, forty years ago,
the first tobacco planters went to Sumatra, they found
a big marshy jungle and many swamps, and they
suffered much from malaria. As the plantations grew,
drainage operations were very carefully undertaken, for
it was found that the finest kinds of tobacco could only
be grown as the result of very careful drainage, and the
suitable drying of the soil ; in consequence, the swamps
had disappeared, and they were now as free from
malaria on the plantations as Holland itself. Malaria

Fig. 20.—SAMAN TREE COVERED WITH WATER-HOLDING MOSQUITO-BREEDING EPIPHYTES (BROMELIACEÆ), TRINIDAD.

[p. 92]

cases were only encountered as the coast line was approached ; it had disappeared from the plantations now spreading over the interior of the island. They were thus able to compare side by side the effect of drainage in stopping malaria, and to see persisting malaria as bad as in the old days in those districts where there was no tobacco planting, and, in consequence, where no drainage had been undertaken.

Cocoa Plantations.—In Grenada it has been found by the medical men that a material decrease in the number of cases of malaria has resulted from the replacement of sugar cane by cocoa plantations. It is necessary for the efficient cultivation of cocoa that the soil should be thoroughly drained, and for this purpose the plantations are intersected by very numerous drainage channels leading from the high grounds to a main channel at the lowest part of the estate. By these means, water never puddles or remains stagnant. Careful cultivation, including drainage undertaken as we have seen in the case of Ismailia, leads both to the increased production of crops and to a diminution of the cases of malaria.

In the case of the sugar-cane fields in British Guiana, intersected as they are by numerous trenches and canals, the anophelines are kept under by the presence of fish, and by flushing.

In the rice fields, although for the most part submerged, small fish appear to be the chief means of keeping in check the production of the anophelines.

Dr. Sergent states that grape-vine planting in

Algeria, necessitating careful drainage, has diminished malaria.

Botanic gardens are very frequently the preserves of the mosquito, for on them ornamental ponds and fountains and innumerable tubs and water-barrels are the rule, and unless these are stocked with small fish they are a fertile source of mosquitos. As previously pointed out, trees and plants may aid to an enormous degree in the production of mosquitos. Tree mosquitos have been conveniently grouped by Dr. Urich in Trinidad into the "rot hole," "bamboo," and "wild pine" groups. Old trees are often honeycombed with decay holes, and in these water collects and mosquitos lay their eggs. When bamboo cane is cut down it is very common for the workmen to leave an internode, in which one or more pints of water can collect and act precisely as a miniature pond. I have already referred to the "wild pine" (*Bromeliaceæ*) which infest trees in enormous numbers, and in the aggregate hold up a great quantity of water. There are in addition numerous other small water-holding plants, such as the Aroideæ, which in towns, if allowed to grow up in neglected places, give rise to a mosquito nuisance in a very short time. Therefore more attention should be given to the question of the care of bush and plants in tropical towns than is usually done at the present time. Bush should be rigorously cut down around towns, and on no account should it be allowed to increase in yards and gardens as is almost invariably the case. Not only does bush hold up water, but it also gives excellent cover to mosquitos and enables them to progress from

FIG. 21.—TOO MUCH BUSH. GEORGETOWN, DEMERARA. THE EFFECT IS TO OBSCURE SUNLIGHT AND FRESH AIR.

p. 94]

point to point. Bush also is one of the chief agents in keeping out fresh air in towns, where fresh air is above all things necessary ; it also forms cover for plague rats and their fleas. By some it is argued that bush helps evaporation. The contrary is the case ; the admission of more air and light would accomplish far more. Plant cultivation in towns also leads to various devices for keeping them moist or protected from ants, and these devices in their turn lead to the breeding of mosquitos. Thus, flower-pot saucers are a very common breeding place of the stegomyia, and so are the antiformicas with which rare plants are protected from the inroads of the umbrella ants. I have found larvæ in them in very numerous instances. And whilst on the subject I would like to draw attention to the very numerous occasions upon which I have found mosquito larvæ, usually those of stegomyia, in glass vases used either for holding cut flowers or, more frequently, for propagating cuttings of the Croton plant; the reason is, of course, that either the water is not changed often enough, or when the water is changed, the larvæ and eggs cling to the roots when the old water is thrown away, and when the fresh water is added the larvæ are as vigorous as ever. Upon one occasion I found a swarm of stegomyia larvæ breeding in a pool that had formed between the buttresses of an old silk-cotton tree. Another not very obvious site for the fostering of mosquito larvæ are the small pools which are found amongst the rocks of a rockbound coast. These, in many instances, come close up to human habitations, as in St. Vincent, and in such cases the domestic mosquito, like the stegomyia, may breed in them. These pockets should be either filled in with concrete or so chiselled that water cannot remain in them. In many of the more low-lying swampy coasts crab-holes occur in enormous numbers in the sandy soil, and in them are bred vast numbers of mosquitos. In fact they constitute the chief nuisance in those houses which are situated near the sea.

Fig. 22.—Collecting crab-hole mosquitos, Bridgetown, Barbados.

CHAPTER X

YELLOW FEVER

DR. BEAUPERTHUY ON TRADITION IN MEDICINE, AND HIS
VIEW ON THE MODE OF TRANSMISSION OF YELLOW
FEVER—HARRISON AND MOXLY ON THE NATURE
OF THE VIRUS OF YELLOW FEVER

In introducing the subject of malaria I have already alluded to the opinions of certain men of great distinction in the medical world who, long before the scientific proof of the relationship of the mosquito to disease, had come to the conclusion that yellow fever was carried by a mosquito. There was, for instance, Surgeon-General Blair, the great authority on yellow fever, who stated in connection with that disease that *"its shifting lines of infection and gyratory movements suggest to the imagination the attributes of insect life"*; and then there was the other great naturalist-physician, Dr. Louis Daniel Beauperthuy, who in no uncertain manner pinned his belief on the power of insects to transmit diseases, and even went so far as to accuse the *"Zancudo bobo"* (the stegomyia), the domestic mosquito, as being the carrier of yellow fever. He was right, but men did not know it; and as his writings

7

have now a very real interest I have reproduced in the
following pages his observations taken from the volume
of collected papers issued by his brother after his death
in 1871. I have left them all in the original French.
Then we come to the modern period (1881) to Dr.
Charles Finlay. He also had spotted the stegomyia,
and his observations proved of the greatest assistance
in directing researches to this insect. Finlay presented
his paper, showing that the mosquito carried the infection
from *man to man*, before the Academy of Sciences of
Havana in 1881. Beauperthuy, it will be remembered,
also believed that it was the domestic mosquito, but
held that its virus was telluric in origin.

There are two parts of Beauperthuy's writings here
reproduced to which I wish to direct the reader's special
attention. One part is that in which he refers to the
hampering effect of tradition in our great profession.
He points out in the history of the disease known as
Scabies the number of centuries it took medical men
before they would confess that scabies was a parasitic
affection, and that, too, in spite of the fact that the
"poor negro" had recognised its parasitic origin. The
other paragraph to which I would direct special attention
is that dealing with the common fly.

Tradition in Medicine

" The profession said," writes Beauperthuy, that "La
gale, la peste, se propageaient, par les inoculations
miasmatiques par contact immédiat ou par les vêtements
ou autres objets touchés par les galeux, par les
pestiférés ; ces mêmes objets pouvaient, après un

certain laps de temps plus ou moins long, occasionner, par leur contact sur des corps sains, la contagion miasmatique. Telles furent les ingénieuses créations que les hommes de l'art imaginèrent à une époque peu avancée de la médecine pour expliquer des phénomènes dont la cause échappait à leur investigation. Presque toutes ces données régissent encore la science actuelle, à l'exception des miasmes contagieux de la gale, qu'il fallut enfin effacer de l'ancien tableau étiologique, pour lui substituer . . . quoi ? Un insecte, un acarien. Linné, Arenzoar et d'autres médecins avaient signalé la sarcopte de la gale comme 'producteur de cette maladie. Le culte voué aux opinions adoptées et consacrées par le temps avait conservé les anciens errements. Il a fallu trois siècles pour arriver à établir un fait aussi facile à vérifier et à faire connaître la véritable cause d'une affection aussi élémentaire que la gale. Grâce à Gales, la gale fut enfin effacée du tableau des maladies vésiculeuses pour ouvrir la série des maladies parasitaires, pour établir à grandpeine une vérité que savaient les nègres de nos colonies, les indigènes de toute l'Amérique du Sud, le vulgaire de tous les pays. Ceux qui voulaient avoir plus de génie que la nature, ignoraient seuls ce fait trivial.

The Mosquito is the Miasm.

" L'absence d'insectes tipulaires pendant l'hiver explique pourquoi dans cette saison le voisinage des marais cesse d'être dangereux. Les marais immenses du Nord de l'Europe ne sont point malsains par la même raison. Les marais ne communiquent à l'atmosphère que de l'humidité, et la faible quantité de gaz hydrogène carboné qu'ils exhalent ne produit chez l'homme aucune indisposition dans les régions équatoriales et intertropicales réputées pour leur insalubrité. Ce n'est pas seulement la corruption des eaux qui les rend insalubres, mais la présence des tipulaires.

"Pendant la saison de la sécheresse, défavorable aux tipulaires, les fièvres cessent au Sénégal, dans les plaines de l'Apure, de Caracas et de la Guyane. Elles sévirent pendant la saison des pluies, qui est celle de la production des tipulaires. Les affections qu'elles occasionnent prennent plus de gravité lorsque les tipulaires *pullulent* dans les eaux stagnantes et corrompues.

"Arenzoar avait fait connaître, depuis trois siècles, l'acarus qui produit la gale; il en avait indiqué la provenance. Linné signala de nouveau l'existence de l'acarus scabiei aux médecins; mais l'existence de l'acarus gênait les théories régnantes. A quoi bon admettre une vérité nouvelle, isolée, qui menace de renverser tout un système médical merveilleusement inventé et répondant à presque toutes les nécessités, un peu plus ou un peu moins, de la science? Pourquoi déranger tout un édifice intellectuel pour y introduire une innovation dégradante pour l'art et dangereuse pour les dogmes enseignés par le maître et soutenus par d'innombrables disciples?"

Tradition said:

"Les émanations marécageuse s se répandent avec plus d'énergie le soir que dans le reste de la journée. C'est aussi à ces heures que les insectes tipulifères sont plus actifs. Les habitants des pays marécageux sont moins exposés que les étrangers à contracter la fièvre intermittente. Comme si les émanations marécageuses séviraient avec moins d'énergie sur les organes soumis habituellement à leur influence, que sur ceux qui la ressentent pour la première fois.

" La mouche commune et autres petits diptères qui s'attachent aux ulcères, aux substances excrémentitielles et putrides, sont sujets au parasitisme des acariens : c'est un fait d'une grande généralité. Les mouches communes qui s'attachent avec une ténacité si incommode aux lèvres et aux orifices du nez, sont des insectes malades, comme l'atteste leur état de maigreur : elles cherchent leur soulagement en déposant les germes de leur affection sur les téguments, à l'origine des membranes muqueuses. Après avoir pressé ces insectes entre deux verres de manière à leur ôter la vie, on les soumet, après trois ou quatre jours dans ces climats, à l'observation microscopique : on ne tarde pas à apercevoir des acarus adultes qui s'échappent de leurs cavités abdominales et se fixent aux organes extérieurs. Ces observations sont faciles à faire et ne demandent qu'un peu de soin.

How Flies Carry Disease

" Les acariens se transportent sur l'enveloppe tégumentaire de l'homme et des animaux par locomotion ; mais cette voie est le moins ordinaire. Ce sont les mouches domestiques, auxquelles ils s'attachent, qui leur servent le plus habituellement de véhicule. Ces diptères, attirés par les matières en décomposition sur lesquelles vivent les acariens, sont fréquemment envahis par eux et les transportent, soit sur l'homme, soit sur les objets qui l'entourent. On reconnaît les mouches atteintes de ces parasites à leur apparence maladive, à leur importunité et à l'obstination qu'elles mettent à se poser au pourtour des ouvertures des membranes muqueuses de l'homme et des animaux. Elles transportent sur ces orifices les acariens qui les tourmentent et s'en débarrassent au préjudice du nouvel hôte qui les reçoit. La présence de ces insectes sur les lèvres et au bord des narines occasionne une vive démangeaison et des boutons vésiculeux, semblables à des boutons de gale, dont l'éruption s'accompagne d'une réaction fébrile éphémère. Ces éruptions phycténoides partielles sont connues sous les noms *d'herpès labialis, praeputialis, nasalis,* etc.

How Malaria, Yellow Fever, etc., are Carried

" Les fièvres intermittentes, rémittentes et perni- cieuses, ainsi que la fièvre jaune, le choléra morbus et les accidents causés par les serpents et autres animaux venimeux, reconnaissent pour cause un virus animal ou végéto-animal dont l'introduction dans l'organisme humain se fait par voie d'inoculation. Les fluides ou virus inoculés déterminent, après une période d'incuba- tion plus ou moins longue, des symptômes nerveux dans le principe et plus tard une infection putride du sang et des autres fluides de l'économie, portant le trouble dans la circulation, la respiration, la digestion et toutes les autres fonctions.

" Les fièvres intermittentes sont graves en raison du développement des insectes tipulaires, et ces fièvres cessent d'exister ou perdent beaucoup de leur intensité dans les fôrets qui par suite de leur altitude nourrissent peu de ces insectes, quelles que soient les masses de matières végétales qui y subissent la décomposition putride.

" Les Indiens, pour se garantir des fièvres, font usage de certains préservatifs, et, lorsqu'ils habitent leurs vallées malsaines, de brasiers allumés à l'entrée de leurs cabanes pendant la nuit. Ce moyen est très efficace pour chasser les insectes tipulaires. Ils le négligent lorsqu'ils voyagent dans d'autres localités.

" De tous les moyens en usage pour se préserver de l'action énervante occasionnée par les piqûres des insectes tipulaires, le plus efficace est celui qu'emploient les Indiens, consistant à se frotter la peau avec des substances huileuses. Il est vrai que leur peau reste sans défense contre l'introduction de l'aiguillon de ces insectes ; mais le contact d'une substance grasse dans l'intérieur du tube capillaire qui sert à l'inoculation du venin, suffit pour obstruer ce conduit et s'opposer à l'instillation du virus sécrété par les glandes salivaires de l'insecte : la piqûre alors perd toutes ses propriétés délétères et se réduit à une simple incommodité qui n'a rien de préjudiciable pour la santé et n'altère en rien la composition du sang.

" L'expression de serpents ailés employée par Hérodote est fort applicable aux insectes tipulaires et à l'action de leurs piqûres sur l'économie humaine. Tant il est vrai de dire que la vérité apparaissait aux anciens jusque dans les fables.

" La fièvre jaune atteignit un degré de malignité peu commun. L'épidémie s'étendit sur les Indiens comme sur les Européens, sans distinction de classes. Les nègres eux-mêmes ne furent pas exemptés. Elle atteignait depuis les enfants de quatre ans jusqu'aux hommes de l'âge le plus avancé ; M. Manuel Artiz, vieillard presque centenaire, fut attaqué du typhus amaril. Je lui assurai qu'il accomplirait le siècle, et j'eus le bonheur de lui tenir parole.

" Dans la mission que j'avais à remplir, j'apportais le fruit de quatorze années d'observations faites au microscope sur les altérations du sang et des autres fluides de l'économie animale dans les fièvres de tous les types.

" Ces observations, faites dans les régions équinoxiales et intertropicales, me furent d'un grand secours pour reconnaître la cause de la fièvre jaune, et les moyens propres à combattre cette terrible maladie. Quant à mes travaux sur l'étiologie de la fièvre jaune, je m'abstiendrai pour le moment de les livrer à la publicité. Mes recherches à cet égard font partie d'un grand travail, dont les résultats offrent des faits tellement nouveaux, et si éloignés des doctrines reçues, que je ne dois pas les présenter à la publicité sans apporter à leur appui les démonstrations les plus évidentes. Du reste, j'envoie à l'Académie des Sciences de Paris une lettre scellée qui renferme le résumé des observations que j'ai faites jusqu'ici et dont le but est de m'assurer à toute éventualité la priorité de mes découvertes sur la cause des fièvres en général. Quant à la méthode curative que j'ai employée et qui a également réussie sur les Européens et sur les indigènes atteints de la fièvre jaune, je ne crains pas de la publier. Ces faits sont faciles à observer et tout médecin intelligent et de bonne foi qui usera, sans restriction, de mes préceptes contre le typhus amaril, obtiendra les résultats que j'ai obtenus moi-même.

" On ne peut considérer la fièvre jaune comme une affection contagieuse. Les causes de cette maladie se développent dans des conditions climatériques leur permettant de s'étendre à la fois ou successivement sur plusieurs localités. Ces conditions sont : l'élévation de la température, l'humidité, le voisinage des cours d'eau, les lagunes, le peu d'élévation du sol au-dessus du niveau de la mer. Ces conditions sont celles qui favorisent le développement des insectes tipulaires.

" Les tipules introduisent dans la peau leur suçoir, composé d'un aiguillon canalisé piquant et de deux scies latérales ; ils instillent dans la plaie une liqueur venimeuse qui a des propriétés identiques à celles du venin des serpents à crochets. Il ramollit les globules du sang, détermine la rupture de leurs membranes tégumentaires, dissout la partie parenchymateuse, facilite le mélange de la matière colorante avec le sérum. Cette action est en quelque sorte instantanée, comme le démontre l'examen microscopique, puisque le sang absorbé par ces insectes, au moment même de la succion, ne présente pas de globules. Cette action dissolvante paraît faciliter le passage du fluide sanguin dans le conduit capillaire du suçoir. Si l'insecte est interrompu dans l'opération de la succion, tout le venin reste dans la plaie et produit une plus vive démangeaison que lorsqu'une grande partie du fluide venimeux est repompée avec le sang. On attribue sans motif le prurit à la rupture de l'aiguillon ; cet aiguillon est une substance cornée élastique, dont je n'ai jamais observé la rupture dans mes nombreuses observations.

" Les agents de cette infection présentent un grand nombre de variétés qui ne sont pas toutes nuisibles au même degré. La variété *zancudo bobo*, à pattes rayées de blanc, est en quelque sorte l'espèce domestique. Elle est la plus commune et sa piqûre est inoffensive comparativement à celle des autres espèces. . Le puyon est le plus gros et le plus venimeux ; il produit une gale ; son aiguillon est bifurqué à son extrémité ; sa piqûre, dans les cas les plus favorables, où le venin n'est pas absorbé dans l'économie, détermine une irritation locale qui présente la forme d'un bouton prurigineux semblable au scabies purulent, mais nullement contagieux. C'est surtout les enfants qu'il attaque. L'étendue du foyer de la suppuration rend difficile les recherches qui tendent à découvrir l'existence du sarcopte dans ces vésicules.

" Que sont les matières pélagiques dont les tipulaires se nourrissent, sinon des substances animales phosphorescentes comme la chair des poissons ? Qu'y a-t-il d'étrange que l'instillation dans le corps de l'homme de ces substances à l'état putride produise des désordres très graves ? M. Magendie n'a-t-il pas prouvé que quelques gouttes d'eau de poisson pourri, introduites dans le sang des animaux, déterminaient en peu d'heures des symptômes analogues à ceux du typhus et la fièvre jaune ? N'est-ce pas, en effet, une instillation de poison en putréfaction que versent ces insectes sous la peau et dans le tissu cellulaire de l'homme ?

" Les animalcules de la fièvre jaune se meuvent dans toutes les directions, remontant le courant, et sont doués d'un mouvement de giration de droite à gauche et de gauche à droite. Une très petite quantité de sulfate de quinine mélangée avec le liquide, paralyse instantanément l'action des animalcules. Ils sont entraînés par le cours du liquide sans manifester aucun mouvement."

(Cet article a été publié dans la *Gazette officielle de Cumaná*, le 23 mai 1854, no. 57.)

Was Yellow Fever Contagious or Not ?

Just as in the case of malaria so in the case of yellow fever, much controversy and speculation took place as to whether the disease could be passed on from man to man, either by contact or through the secretions, or through the clothes. So two schools arose in the eighteenth century, the contagionists and the non-contagionists. It was chiefly with a view of getting information upon this vexed subject that the 1852 Commission was appointed, and upon its findings the quarantine laws of the period *re* yellow fever were modified where necessary. As a result of their deliberations the Committee reported as follows:

"That epidemics are preceded by individual and sporadic cases, which cases likewise occur in seasons when no epidemics prevail. That epidemics are very often local, and limited to one part of a town. That epidemics do not spread by gradual progression, but often skip over certain adjacent districts. That in an epidemic the most rigid seclusion affords no protection. That great success attends removal to a non-infected locality. That the exciting cause, whatever it is, is local and endemic. That the means of protection from Yellow Fever are not quarantine restrictions and sanitary cordons but sanitary works and operations having for their object the removal of the several localising conditions.

(*Signed*) "SHAFTESBURY,
"EDWIN CHADWICK,
"T. SOUTHWOOD SMITH.
"WHITEHALL, 7 *April* 1852"

They therefore were decided that yellow fever was not contagious. Blair held the same view strongly. He went so far as to inoculate the conjunctiva of healthy persons with the mucus taken from the conjunctiva of persons suffering from yellow fever—in no instance was yellow fever contracted. He mentions numerous cases where nurses had become smeared with the black vomit of patients and suffered no ill effect, also numerous cases in which the wives of yellow fever patients slept in the same bed, or cases in which a patient, through lack of space, was placed in the cot newly vacated by a yellow fever case that had died. In no instance was yellow fever contracted.

In 1793 Dr. Firth of Philadelphia inoculated his arm with the blood taken from a yellow fever patient. He also drank some of the black vomit. No ill effect followed. According to Professor Harrison,[1] a Dr. May dropped some black vomit into his eyes and did not get the fever. Since that period all these experiments, with many more besides, have been re-made, with the like negative effect, showing that the secretions, the bedding, and the clothes did not convey infection. But how, then, was the infection conveyed? Beauperthuy, as we have seen, tried to explain it, and succeeded half way—the mosquito conveyed the virus, but he failed to observe that the mosquito got its virus from infected man. He supposed that it obtained it from decomposing matter. Just as Ross furnished the clue in the case of the anophelines, so Reed, Carroll, Agramonte, and Lazear solved the question in the case of the stegomyia. Beauperthuy's contention that the mosquito obtained its poison from the soil fitted in with the views then firmly held of the local origin of the disease. It was noted over and over again how the disease clung to certain places and houses. With the view of throwing light upon the local origin of the disease, more especially in the case of graveyards which

[1] *Loc. cit.*

had been used to bury yellow fever cases, Professor
Harrison, now of British Guiana, and Mr. Sutton
Moxly, Chaplain of the Forces, both then in Barbados,
undertook a series of experiments to test by inoculation
in the lower animals whether the mould of yellow fever
graves was infective or not. The experiments were
also an answer to observations made by Dr. Freire of
Rio, to the effect that the soil from burials spread the
disease. Harrison and Moxly's experiments showed
that so far as small animals were concerned the soil
was non-infectious.

The most interesting observation of these two early
investigators was the following pregnant statement :

" The theory that we believe, in view of all the
apparently contradictory facts of the case, to be the
most reasonable, and that, if not generally accepted
now, will be when the history of the disease is
thoroughly known, and when the apparently contradictory facts are compared, and given each their due
weight, is that yellow fever is a highly contagious
disease, but that the germs, whatever they may be,
require some time and suitable opportunity for their
development before they can reproduce themselves in
another body ; and that thus the disease is not at least
generally communicable from a sick person to another
who may be in ever so close proximity to him.'

Surely this is an extraordinary coincidence—Beauperthuy certain that it was a mosquito that transferred the poison, Harrison equally convinced that that
poison required some time and suitable opportunity
to develop itself outside the body before it could infect.

Yes! British Guiana can compete on equal terms with Cuba for the honour of having paved the way to the epoch-making discovery, and all honour to the great clinician and the young professor and his clerical companion who, with the simplest instruments, got so near the truth. L. H. R. Carter, of the Marine Hospital Service, had also drawn attention to the curious " extrinsic " period of incubation of yellow fever, that is to say, to the remarkable fact that an interval existed between infected and secondary cases— the interval being, as we now know, the latent period which the virus passes in the stegomyia. It is clear that Harrison and Carter were both thinking alike.

CHAPTER XI

FASCINATING as is the study of malaria, both historically and scientifically, nevertheless that of yellow fever is even still more so, as I shall endeavour to show.

Whilst we read how malaria dogged the footsteps of our forces in the Netherlands, so yellow fever was the disease in the days of the buccaneers, and later of our regular troops at a period in our history when we were engaged in conquering in the West Indies and on the Spanish Main, which time and time again swept our pioneers and soldiers away just as so many flies. Before we had ventured into these waters the terror of yellow fever was well known to the Spanish, Portuguese, French, and Dutch settlers ; it was recognised as the " *disease of the Conquistadores.*"

How often, in wandering through the West Indies, one meets with an obelisk or an isolated tombstone or a disused churchyard, all telling how our own conquistadores, our own soldiers, met their death, not at the hands of a warlike enemy, but, as we now

111

know, vanquished by the sting of an insignificant insect ; and thousands so perished, as the following official narratives attest.

Blair, in an account of the yellow fever epidemic of Georgetown, 1850, quotes as follows from the Report of the Medical Inspector of the West Indian Command for the years 1837–41.

" About the end of August fever began to appear amongst the non-commissioned officers and privates : out of 32 attacked, 15 died. Intermittent fever was at the same time very prevalent : 1,435 cases came under treatment.

" In Trinidad, in May 1838, fever occurred among the troops at St. James's and St. Joseph's : 15 died out of 109 treated. A draft of young Irishmen, just then arrived, suffered most.

" In Dominica this year (1837), out of 65 cases of yellow fever admitted into the hospital, 21 died. Nearly all the officers had the disease and died. In this epidemic, hæmorrhage from the gums and throat was common ; black vomit set in about thirteen hours before death.

" In Trinidad, 1837, at St. Joseph's, 19 men of the detachment there died of fever.

" Grenada about the same time was severely visited by fever.

" At Port Frederick, out of 14 men of the Royal Artillery 11 were attacked, of whom 6 died. At Richmond Hill, out of 207 of the 70th Regiment, 61 were attacked, 14 died. Fever raged amongst the civil population, both white and black ; even the acclimatised by no means escaped ; the crews of the shipping suffered severely.

" In Barbados, 1837–8, in November and December, yellow fever prevailed amongst the inhabitants of Bridgetown and proved very fatal. The troops then were healthy. In the beginning of January, 1839, the disease appeared in the 52nd Regiment, which in the November preceding had arrived from Gibraltar; of 37 admitted into hospital 6 died. The officers of the regiment suffered in a greater proportion. Of 10 attacked 3 died; 12 was the whole number in barracks. It is remarkable that every individual who had any duty to perform requiring his presence in the orderly room, which was in the officers' barracks (previously considered healthy), was attacked with fever; and also that few escaped who occupied the adjoining lower rooms; thus, of 24 persons connected with this part of the building, only 2 females and 4 young children escaped the disease. The building was vacated, the floor taken up—nothing offensive was found underneath.

" In the quarter ending June 30th there was an average of 39 deaths out of every 123 cases. The inhabitants at the time were reported healthy, as also the seamen and the troops in Berbice and at the outstations. The weather was described as particularly fine.   •

" In St. Vincent, in the same quarter, yellow fever was very destructive amongst the troops; out of 310 (the total strength of the white troops) 241 cases occurred, 54 died; out of 18 officers, the whole in the garrison, 9 were attacked, 4 died.

" In St. Lucia, from the middle of August to the end of September, the troops at Morne Fortuné suffered from fever; out of 134 white troops 93 were attacked, 20 died. The inhabitants suffered even more; amongst

8

them the disease appeared in the early part of July. The weather was unusually dry and hot. About the same time fever was severe and destructive amongst the inhabitants of St. John's, Antigua. The troops in the island escaped the disease.

"In the quarter ending December 31, 1839, fever prevailed amongst the troops in Barbados; it was fatal, and obtained chiefly in the brick barracks. It first appeared amongst the respectable inhabitants in the early part of October, and about the end of the month became prevalent in the garrison. The hospital sergeant and orderlies of the 52nd Regiment were amongst the first taken ill; then the families of the married men; then the troops in the barracks. The disease broke out amongst the troops on the ships, and even in Trinidad (March 1846) fever prevailed; 402 cases occurred, 13 died.

"In Tobago, during the same quarter (1846), 62 were attacked with fever out of 71, 8 died.

"In St. Kitts, out of 8 attacked 4 died.

"In the same year 7 fatal cases of fever occurred amongst the troops in Berbice, 5 in Trinidad, 24 in St. Kitts, out of 90 attacked.

"In the following quarter (1840), at St. Kitts, there were 10 deaths from fever out of a garrison of 33 attacked; the civil inhabitants suffered as well as the troops. During the twelve months ending March 31, the deaths from fever at Brimstone Hill, St. Kitts, were 49, which was a large proportion of the garrison."

Again, in the year 1847, during a severe epidemic in Georgetown, Demerara, Surgeon-General Blair wrote:

"Within the trenches aquatic larvæ and exuviæ abounded, and over them clouds of mosquitos and

sandflies.   Such was the condition of the neighbourhood of the Military Grounds during the epidemic.
These particulars were noted by me more especially
in 1840, in consequence of a reference being made to
me by His Excellency the Governor, with a view to
reply to a dispatch from the Right Hon. the Secretary
at War regarding the question why in a few months
69 *per cent. of all the white troops had perished.*   In
close proximity and to leeward of the marsh stood the
Military Hospital.   It is said that almost every case
admitted to this hospital during the epidemic became
yellow fever, no matter what the ailment on admission ;
and it ultimately became such a terror to the soldiers
that the utmost difficulty was experienced in persuading
them to enter it when sick."

And again we read :

" Fergusson tells us how the troops at St. Domingo,
after disembarking, one and all suffered.   At the commencement of the epidemic a census was taken of the
inhabitants, and they and the newly arrived soldiers
totalled equal numbers at the conclusion of the epidemic.
1,500 soldiers—that is, the original complement of the
men—had perished.   No wonder we read about a general
who lost his reason when he saw, in spite of all his
efforts for their wellbeing, his men struck down by
hundreds by invisible bullets.   In the words of Blair,
so persistently did yellow fever dog the footsteps of the
early European pioneers, whether on plunder or conquest bent, that it seemed as if the European carried
something upon his person which, coming in contact
with the tropical atmosphere, lit up a conflagration.
The moment, wrote Prescott, a town is founded, or a

commercial centre created, it is certain to cause the explosion of the latent malignity of the poison in the air."

No wonder, then, that around such a disease, magic and mystery were freely invoked to account for it. Yes, and little wonder that to-day may still be found surviving some old practitioners of medicine who cannot shake the *juju* off and will take you to see a "yellow fever house"—a house haunted with the yellow fever pestilential miasm of former generations, and in which, if you reside, you will surely get yellow fever !

Just as in the case of malaria, so in this disease : miasms—the chemical reactions arising from the union of salt water with fresh—were considered an ideal explanation, for it fitted in with appearances. Our tropical seaports were attacked by yellow fever, and in these tropical seaports it invariably happened that the incoming salt-water tides met with the outflowing fresh water of the tropical river or the water of the lagoon; and it was to that natural phenomenon that wise men attributed a chemical reaction and the engendering of a " fibrilifying influence." The " fibrilifying influence " was described as a terrestrial poison which a high atmospheric heat generates amongst the newly arrived. The frequent outbreak of yellow fever on board ships led to a host of theories which are amongst the most absurd of the modern period of the history of medicine, only finding their parallel away back in the days of alchemy and witchcraft. The outbreaks on board ship were described as spontaneous. The cargo was blamed; it might have been green logs from Sierra Leone or logwood from Honduras. But the majority of authorities laid the blame to ballast, especially shingles, gravel, mud or sand. The ballast was more often than not wet when put in, or made so by the drippings from the fresh-water tanks stored on board. The pestiferous emanations from bilge water, mixed with the ballast in all the forms in which it was encountered in the days of sailing ships, were supposed to be the chief cause, and very numerous examples of this are given in the "Report on Yellow Fever," General Board of Health, London, 1852. Quite recently Dr. Manning of Barbados has reviewed a considerable number of these instances to support the view which he shares, and which, as we now see, were the views of the school of miasms, fibrilifying influences, concatenations, in the days before science had given us the true explanation. The persistence of views like these to-day shows in a very marked degree how hard it is to kill tradition and superstition in our profession. The explanation of all these so-called "spontaneous" outbreaks on board ship has been admirably given by Dr. Le Bœuf and by other American writers of the past few years. A little thought will show at once that yellow fever has almost disappeared from ships since wooden vessels were replaced by iron steamships. In the old days before a steam condensing plant, fresh water was carried in numerous casks which were more often than not leaky, the fresh water was taken in at the ports of call, and no doubt contained innumerable stegomyia larvæ and eggs which developed during the voyage into the winged insect. The ship then became like a house in a yellow fever town ; the particular species of mosquito—the stegomyia—was there. All then that was necessary to light up an epidemic on board was that a labourer or some one from shore suffering from the disease should come aboard, or that a member of the ship's crew should go ashore and contract the disease. Soon after the ship would sail and he would naturally develop the disease, and presently every mosquito in the whole ship would become infected ; and then most of the crew would be down with yellow fever. There is no necessity to search for a miasm nor to ask us to discover a sea mosquito, as Dr. Manning suggests, for an explanation of this now well-known fact. That the stegomyia can and does develop in fresh water on shipboard in warm latitudes as easily as it can ashore is now well known, and if it can transmit yellow fever ashore, it certainly can do so on board ship, which is to all intents and purposes a floating house. But no, in spite of all these explanations, tradition and yellow fever houses and *juju* still cling.

Although yellow fever and malaria have been' usually bracketed close to one another (and as we now know there was a reason for so doing, for they are both mosquito-carried), yet Blair recognised the very great difference which existed between malaria and yellow fever from the point of view of ætiology, for he states :

" It is remarkable that some of the most destructive outbreaks of yellow fever have occurred amongst the troops at stations where intermittent fever is almost unknown as indigenous : for instance, Brimstone Hill in St. Kitts ; Fort Charlotte in St. Vincent ; St. Ann in Barbados ; and *vice versâ*, those colonies in which ague are most common have been least frequently visited by yellow fever—*e.g.* Demerara and Berbice."

The reason for this difference is now quite clear. The life-story of the anopheles and the stegomyia is quite different; the one is an earth-pool breeder, the other a domestic drinking-water-barrel or odd drinking-water-receptacle breeder. The one therefore is much dependent upon the rains or upon permanent springs and marshes, the other chiefly dependent upon the hand of man, who provides the receptacle and fills it with the drinking water necessary for the use of his household.

History.—There is every reason for supposing that yellow fever is one of the very old diseases of mankind in the New World. It is stated that it was known to the Aztecs under the name of *matlazahualt*, and according to Humboldt it existed as early as the eleventh century.

Amongst old Spanish writers who refer to this disease may be mentioned Oviedo, who in his " Historia General de las Indias " describes the great mortality among the followers of Columbus in 1494. This mortality he attributes to the humidity of St. Domingo, but in every probability it was yellow fever. So bad were the reports which reached Spain, that Ferdinand V. had to send out 300 convicts to the island as there were no volunteers.

Columbus in 1498, in writing to the King of Spain upon the sickness of his men, attributed their illness to " peculiarities in the air and water " in the new land. No doubt the peculiarity was the mosquito.

In the sixteenth century yellow fever is said to have decimated the Mexicans. But the first authentic history of an epidemic of yellow fever was furnished by Jean Terreyra de Rosa at Olinda in Brazil in the year 1687.

Père Dutertre, 1635, appears to have been the first to furnish details of the symptoms and progress of the disease in the West Indies. He regarded it as a new disease.

Père Labat, whose name is well known in connection with yellow fever, found on landing in Martinique in the year 1649, the disease raging in the island, the monks of the religious order stationed there being severely afflicted. The learned father stated that the disease was called " the Maladie de Siam," because in Martinique they supposed that it was imported from Siam by the ship *Oriflamme*. As, however, this ship called at Brazilian ports on the voyage, it is much more probable that either the crew became infected there or that infected mosquitos were carried away. According to Bancroft the disease existed in St. Domingo in 1731. Old writers upon yellow fever frequently refer to the West Coast of Africa as being the original source of the disease.[1]

Thus Dr. Chisholm believed that yellow fever was

[1] Dr. Le Bœuf, in interesting notes on "History of Yellow Fever," published in the New Orleans *Medical and Surgical Journal*, 1905.

first introduced into the West Indies in 1793, when Grenada became infected from the remarkable ship *Hankey*, which had come from Bulam in West Africa. On account of this supposed origin of yellow fever it is sometimes called Bulam fever. Evidence, however, points the other way,—that in fact it was a very prevalent disease in the New World, stretching from Mexico down through Central America to Brazil. Brazil appears, then, to have been the centre from which it radiated out to the West Indies. As I have stated before, the early Conquistadores suffered from it, the Latin races of the Old World being therefore the first to make its acquaintance during the time they were occupied in pushing civilisation into the then newly discovered continent.

In Cuba yellow fever was probably known as the Pest or Epidemic of Havana as early as 1620. The first authentic description of the black vomit in Havana was furnished by Dr. Thomas Romay in the year 1761.

In the beginning of the eighteenth century the disease, from its appearance in various parts of Spanish America under the name of *vomito prieto*, attracted much attention, and it is particularly referred to by the historian Ulloa, who resided for some years in that country. The word *prieto* appears to be the Portuguese or nearly obsolete Spanish term for black. In Spanish the word *negro* is now universally substituted. A small pamphlet of sixty-two pages by a Dr. Gastelbondo, written at Carthagena (S.A.) in 1753 and printed at Madrid in 1755, was probably the first work *ex professo* on the black vomit as it appeared in South

America. He gives his experience of the disease during forty years. He says on the title page that he is about to write about a disease of frequent occurrence in that part of the world, mentions change of climate and mode of living among some of the causes of the disease in new-comers, and says that the natives of Carthagena, Vera Cruz, etc., were not subject to attacks of the true black vomit fever, though liable to the " Chapetonada," a disease resembling it in some respects.

From its home in Central and South America we find yellow fever carried into other latitudes along the trade routes or by the returning soldiers. Time was when Baltimore, Philadelphia, Boston, and the Southern States of Mississippi, Louisiana, Tennessee were ravaged by yellow fever ; this was the period when there was an extensive and unguarded trade intercourse with the West Indies and Central America. A mortality of 50 to 60 per cent. of the population was often recorded in those days.

" It seems strange," writes Gilkrest, referring to the epidemic at Cadiz, " that writers should have over-looked the remarkable epidemics at that place in the years 1730, 1731, and 1736, recorded by different authorities, the two first being very particularly noticed by Villalba in his curious work ' Epidemilogia Española.' It seems equally extraordinary that those writers should have overlooked the black vomit epidemic which pre-vailed in Spain previous to those of Cadiz and Malaga."

Race Susceptibility.—The Latin races are perhaps those which are considered to be the most liable to yellow fever. Thus in British Guiana Dr. Walbridge gave it as his opinion that the most predisposed were the Norwegians, Danes, Germans, and Portuguese, the latter being so greatly predisposed that their emigration from Madeira was prohibited for a time. One of the reasons why the Latin races are regarded as more susceptible comes no doubt from the fact that these races inhabit the yellow fever zones. They were the first settlers and were the first to suffer. But in the days when large bodies of British troops were stationed in the West Indies, they suffered to a terrible extent, as we have already seen. There may, however, be some reason for the Latin races appearing to suffer more than the other races, and that is this: in my experience I have obtained the impression that in the houses, yards, and gardens kept by the Portuguese, Spanish or French, there are more water-containers of all kinds for storing the drinking water and washing water for the clothes, water for the poultry and domestic animals. The houses of the Latin people appear to me always to have more children, domestic animals, chickens, etc., about than the houses of the natives or those of the English residents. So, therefore, the question may be simply that of providing the largest number of breeding places, and, reasoning from the analogy of fleas and rats, this seems to be the simplest explanation.

The black race has been said to enjoy a remarkable immunity. This is, however, far from the case. The greatest observers have pointed out how time and time again they suffer equally with the white races; the most recent epidemic in Barbados is an example of this. Examples are also cited by Blair and in the 1852 Commission's Report.

From the earliest times yellow fever has been described as the disease of the unacclimatised, the disease of the new arrival; for that very reason it was thought that as every new arrival must sooner or later get it, the sooner it was got over the better, and with this kind of reasoning the native inhabitants folded their arms and did nothing. It was the young soldiers and merchants who suffered in the old days, and to-day in many parts of the world, as in the Amazon, it is the young merchants who fall to the disease.

The explanation is that the native, be he black or white, has no natural immunity, but he has acquired immunity through having had an attack of the disease, most probably in childhood. He survives, and is in consequence immune. When, therefore, a case of yellow fever is imported into a district and infects the stegomyias, those who succumb are naturally the non-immunes, that is, the new arrivals. But let it be now observed that with the increase of sanitation and the diminution of mosquitos, brought about as described in a previous chapter, yellow fever has become rarer in the yellow fever zone of the world. This means that the immunising process which used to occur in the old days no longer takes place now, and every year adds to the number of native non-immunes ; they no longer get the opportunity of acquiring the disease. In other words, the black has now become as susceptible as the latest white arrival to yellow fever. This is, at any rate, my interpretation of why the native Barbadian is suffering from yellow fever equally with the new arrivals.

Periodicity.—This has been referred to by many writers, and it is often stated that in the case of Barbados the island is visited at intervals of thirteen years. Here again the coincidence is probably dependent upon the creation of a larger susceptible population during the interval of freedom from disease, the immunes having diminished in the meantime through natural causes, as by death.

CHAPTER XII

YELLOW FEVER

SCIENTIFIC FACTS RECORDED IN CONNECTION WITH YELLOW FEVER

YELLOW fever is an exceedingly good example of a disease in which, although up to date the actual parasite or agent which produces the disease has not been conclusively demonstrated as in the case of malaria, sleeping sickness, Malta fever, tuberculosis, and numerous other infectious diseases, nevertheless certain other facts in connection with the disease have been so convincingly proved that from the administrative side, that is from the prophylaxis point of view, there is not the trace of a doubt as to how the disease can be prevented or what are the conditions which make it quite impossible for it to spread.

The prevention of yellow fever is one of the most brilliant triumphs of modern prophylaxis. The foundation of exact yellow fever prophylaxis was laid in June 1900 by Army Surgeons Reed, Carroll, Agra-

FIG. 23.—A PROPERLY SCREENED CISTERN, NEW ORLEANS.

p. 126]

monte, and Lazear, who were sent to Cuba to study yellow fever. In Havana these observers found that already Dr. C. J. Finlay had, as early as 1881, enunciated the theory in no uncertain manner of the propagation of yellow fever by the mosquito; and, influenced both by this fact and, as they state, also by the brilliant work of Ross and the Italian observers in connection with the propagation of malaria by the mosquito, as well as by certain observations of Carter, they determined to experimentally investigate this line of research. The results obtained by them were most conclusive. In the same year the Liverpool School of Tropical Medicine dispatched Drs. Walter Myers and Durham to study the disease at Para; France followed immediately (late in 1901) with an expedition composed of Drs. Marchoux, Salimbini, and Simond, which made Rio its headquarters. In 1903 a yellow fever working party composed of Rosenau, Beyer, Parker, Pothier, and Francis was sent by the Public Health and Marine Hospital Service to study the transmission of yellow fever at Vera Cruz. Lastly, in 1905 the Liverpool School of Tropical Medicine established for a second time a Yellow Fever Laboratory at Para under the direction of Dr. Thomas, assisted by Dr. Breinl. The conclusions arrived at by these commissions, as well as by Dr. Guiteras in Havana and Drs. Lutz, Ribas, Barreto de Barros, and Rodriques in Brazil, have all fully confirmed the original observations of Reed, Agramonte, Carroll, and Lazear, and have proved that the *Stegomyia calopus* is the sole transmitter of the disease. The

enthusiasm and devotion of this army of workers are
shown by the fact that a very large number of the
workers suffered themselves from the disease, and
that Walter Myers and Lazear succumbed.　Reed,
one of the most brilliant of this group, unfortunately
died at Washington from appendicitis in 1902, hardly
before he had had time to witness the beneficial results
of his remarkable labours.　For although no observer
succeeded in microscopically demonstrating the parasite,
whatever it may be, they proved firstly, as others had
done, that neither the vomit nor the clothes of the
patient were infective; they further proved (and this
was new) that the blood of the patient only contained
the virus five days after having been infected; and
that if then the patient was bitten by one particular
species of mosquito—viz. the *Stegomyia calopus,* and by
that species alone—that then after a latent period of
three days the stegomyia became itself infected and
was capable of transmitting the disease to man.　I
know of no parallel in the history of medical science
of discoveries which appear at first sight so incredible
and as to which, were it not for the equally marvellous
success which has followed acting upon them, we
might be excused for retaining some measure of
sceptical reserve.

The new doctrine swept away as if by magic the
traditional views, which filled very many volumes,
as to the nature and origin and prevention of yellow
jack.　Yellow fever has, as we have seen, been attributed to droughts and to floods, to the pestilential
"mangrove swamp," to high temperatures, to fœcal

matters, to combinations and concatenations of atmospheric circumstances, to stone ballast, hundreds of tons of which have been disinfected or thrown into the sea—theories every one of which have raised bitter controversies and have been the cause during epidemics of the loss of much valuable time. Even to-day there exists in many parts a very deep-rooted prejudice against excavations and dredgings during certain seasons, notably in the summer months, and works of this nature, in spite of their importance and urgency in preserving the health of the community, are deferred for an old tradition, and that, too, after Havana and the Isthmian Canal Zone have proved the absurdity of it. It demonstrates, however, that the newer facts are not yet fully accepted by a section of the public, and that those measures against yellow fever which have now been proved to be the only ones of avail, are not fully adopted. It is hardly necessary to add that in consequence valuable time is lost, and lives and commerce sacrificed.

When it is remembered that the *Stegomyia calopus* is present throughout the year, and that in consequence a town in the tropics in the yellow fever zone may be as liable to infection in the autumn as in the summer, or in the spring, it is obvious that if the excavated or dredged material contained some poison which inoculated the stegomyia or infected man, it would be as effective in the autumn as in the summer or spring, and dredging or excavations would be equally harmful at any time of the year ; it would be impossible to say, as has been said, when "digging

9

operations might be safely commenced." But there is no scientific evidence whatever, as we have seen, to show that dredged or excavated material is infective, and the prejudice does not appear to me to be shared by the natives. Dredging operations have been blamed as the cause of the outbreak in Belize, but the fact is lost sight of that at the same time the fever had declared itself in the surrounding Republics, and that dredging has been carried on over and over again without any epidemic occurring. I lay stress on this clinging to past beliefs because I am convinced that a great deal of harm is done even at the present time, and that the necessity for active preventive measures is unfortunately not fully realised.

Without a clear and precise knowledge of the method of transmission it is impossible for any authority. to effectively prevent or check a disease like yellow fever, in which scientific precision, thoroughness, and immediate action are essential.

DIFFICULTIES OF COMBATING THE DISEASE IN THE PAST

It can be readily understood from the preceding remarks how hopeless and ineffective were the measures of prevention used in the past, and that, too, in spite of the fact that in the more recent periods Listerian principles of disinfection were applied, carbolic acid and perchloride of mercury being freely used as disinfectants. For instance, although Major Gorgas had, previous to the advent of Reed, Carroll, Agramonte, and Lazear, made a vast change in the sanitary condition of Havana, yellow fever was, nevertheless, not

FIG. 24.—A PROPERLY SCREENED WATER BARREL ON PLANTATION DIAMOND, BRITISH GUIANA.

affected ; it only *ceased after employing methods directed against the mosquito, viz. fumigation, screening, and destroying the breeding places of the larvae.* In Belize, during the recent (1905) epidemic, cases of yellow fever occurred amongst the best-cared-for class of people living in the best residential houses, where the sanitary arrangements were excellent.

In the past, from want of knowledge of the true method of transmission, rigorous house quarantine was enforced in the epidemic of 1878 in New Orleans, and vast quantities of disinfectant were used, clothing and baggage were disinfected or destroyed, but nothing but the frost—a natural means of preventing the activity and breeding of the mosquito—stopped the fever. Ships have been turned away with the dying on board, or subjected for long periods to quarantine, thousands of tons of harmless stone ballast have been thrown overboard or disinfected, lest they should spread contagion.

The flood of new light which was thrown upon the nature of yellow fever soon began to have its effect. The first great application of the new principle of prevention of yellow fever was made at Havana in 1901 by Major Gorgas, under the very able administration of General Wood. The result was a complete success ; it has become historic, and constitutes the example to every town in the yellow fever zone of the truth of the doctrine of the mosquito transmission and the practicability of its application. The example has been followed, under Dr. Cruz in Rio, and Dr. Liceaga in Mexico ; great improvements

have been brought about, but an immense amount
of work still remains to be done. A new stimulus
has, however, now been furnished by the successful
campaign of 1905 in New Orleans, and now in the
Canal Zone, and it is to be hoped that a great deal
of the opposition and apathy still to be met with will
soon give place to hearty co-operation and determination to rid yellow fever countries of a pest which
causes so much suffering and cripples commerce.

THE INFECTED *STEGOMYIA CALOPUS*

A knowledge of the following facts is necessary
to understand the application of the prophylactic
measures which are now employed. The yellow fever
patient is only capable of infecting the stegomyia
during the first few days of the onset of the disease ;
the period usually given is the first three days, although
the French authorities extend the infective period.
The yellow fever cadaver after the first three days
of illness is non-infectious ; in consequence the
separate burial ground for yellow fever cases is need-
lessly harsh, quite unnecessary, and unscientific. *At
no late stage can the yellow fever patient or the
cadaver infect man directly.* In common with many
other non-immunes I was almost daily in the Yellow
Fever Emergency Hospital examining patients and
assisting at post-mortems, but no case of infection ever
occurred amongst us. The well-screened Emergency
Hospital, although crowded with patients and extremely
hot, was, nevertheless, one of the safest places in New

Orleans, because the stegomyia was effectively shut out. No case of direct transmission from the patient to man has ever been recorded. The only means is through the mosquito, as Ross has proved in the case of malaria.

When the stegomyia has taken a meal of blood from a patient in the infective stage, it is not at once capable of transmitting by its bite the virus to a healthy individual. *A very definite number of days must elapse before the mosquito is itself infective, and capable of transmitting the virus; approximately this period is twelve days.*

Therefore, at the termination of the period of incubation in the mosquito, fresh cases of infection may be expected to occur in those living in a house in which the mosquitos were not destroyed.

The symptoms of disease will also not declare themselves in man at once, for, as just seen in the case of the mosquito, an incubation period is also necessary in the case of man, *and the period is usually five days.* Consequently an interval of a little over two weeks usually occurs before secondary cases manifest themselves.

SUMMARY

1. Man suffering from yellow fever after the fifth day is the *reservoir.*

2. From this reservoir one species of mosquito, the *Stegomyia calopus,* becomes infected and after the tenth· day becomes the insect *carrier* or transmitting agent of the disease.

3. The reservoirs and the carriers are both necessary for the spread of the disease.

4. Method of attack.

    (*a*) Prevent entry of reservoirs (quarantine measures, etc.).

    (*b*) Exterminate the carrier (anti-adult mosquito measures, screening, fumigation, etc., anti-larval measures, control of water supply, oiling, drainage).

RATIONALE OF THE CHIEF PREVENTIVE MEASURES

I. To Diminish and Control the Reservoirs, i.e. to Prevent Man suffering from the Disease becoming a Disseminator of the Disease.

1. *Early notification and diagnosis necessary in order to isolate the reservoirs as soon as possible.*

Careful inquiry into the origin of the numerous epidemics all over the yellow fever zone proves conclusively that yellow fever has usually gained a firm foothold before the first cases are notified.

In some Central American ports this will prove for a considerable time to come a perpetual source of danger, for the inhabitants of these districts are likely to be more indifferent to the disease, and therefore to be less careful about notification. No doubt this is also the reason why it is laid such stress upon in the opening articles of the Washington Convention of 1905. Commercial reasons, it is alleged, may sometimes operate to hold back notification, but the numerous bitter lessons have shown that the risk of the losses

brought about by allowing the fever to gain a head
is too great. In a modern city swarming with the
stegomyia a concealed case must sooner or later make
itself manifest, and by the time it does so the total
volume of mosquito infection will be so great that
serious disaster is inevitable. Commercial and civic
authorities now commence to realise this, so that the
danger from suppression of the facts is diminishing.
More often the loss of time in early notification is due
to the fact either that cases of the disease are present
amongst the indigenous inhabitants, or that it breaks
out amongst a particular colony of labourers in a town
or district (such as amongst the Sicilians and Italians in
New Orleans in the year 1905, who do not readily seek
medical advice and are often exceedingly suspicious), or
that early cases are not recognised. In districts where
malaria takes a pernicious form, or where dengue is
common, the difficulties of diagnosis must be greatly
increased, and experience under these circumstances
will be of great value. On the other hand, some other
epidemic may have preceded the yellow fever, and
cases which were in reality yellow fever may have been
placed to the credit of the former.

In large cities, as mentioned in the previous chapter,
a clue that something unusual is happening may be
afforded by analysis of the weekly death returns. A
sudden rise in the number of deaths recorded from
malaria in a month, at a season of the year when
malaria has not occurred in previous years, would be
a very suspicious element. In small towns, however,
such indication would probably be too slight to be

of practical value in putting a community upon its guard.

Where the practitioners themselves have had the advantage of previous experience in the disease there is a greater chance of early notification. But I venture to suggest that experience gained of yellow fever or any other disease twenty or fourteen years previously is not so valuable as experience of the disease acquired since our knowledge of the disease has been very greatly increased. For this reason I urge that it would be wise for one or more of the Government medical officers of any colony to be sent, as occasion arises, to study any particular disease affecting the prosperity of the colony, to some place where the particular disease is common. This is one of the chief reasons why the medical officers of the Marine Hospital Service are of such practical service to the United States.

Of supreme importance also is the necessity of obtaining a post-mortem examination of the first suspicious death. The post-mortem findings are characteristic, and do not need microscopic confirmation.

The notification of yellow fever is rightly regarded as a very serious matter, and a young practitioner will undoubtedly hesitate before he declares. If he has notified, and the case does not turn out to be yellow fever as he supposed, he regards his diagnostic power as open to criticism, both by other doctors and by the patient. If he is dealing with a genuine case, and he hesitates till too late, no fumigation is undertaken to kill the infected mosquitos at the outset, and in the meantime contagion is spread—to make itself felt some twelve days afterwards in the same house or in the vicinity. The situation is unquestionably difficult, and it can only be got over by *friendly inter-reliance* amongst the medical men themselves, and by the encouragement given by the Senior Medical Officer to his juniors not to hesitate to express their difficulties to him nor to think that thereby they suffer in his estimation as careful observers. I am convinced that this is very necessary, as there is evidence that this spirit is not always present.

2. *General screening of the reservoirs by the use of an Isolation Hospital.*

This is a most useful measure because amongst the poor or careless it is very difficult to maintain efficient control without the employment of much elaborate machinery and a considerable expenditure of money.

3. *Isolation by screening the Reservoir.*

A great deal can be done in the direction of preventing the spread of the disease by screening the patient, and so preventing the mosquitos from becoming infected and spreading the disease.

Both with regard to the isolation of the patient and the application of fumigation there is a great want of precision. It is useless for any one to apply these two cardinal preventive measures unless they understand the rôle of the mosquito in the dissemination of the disease. The infected mosquitos have to be destroyed both in the house of the patient and often in the adjoining blocks, and the patient must be so placed that no mosquitos can gain access to him. Those who are familiar with the habits of mosquitos know that it is not an easy task to bring about their thorough destruction in living-houses, and that fumigation must be applied with absolute thoroughness to all parts of the house, closets, and outhouses ; and that to do this the house, closets, and outhouses must be so completely sealed that a mosquito cannot get away through any chink. Again, those familiar with mosquitos know that it is very difficult to keep them out of screened rooms, unless the screening is well done and the doors are of the proper kind. It is only by the rigid application of these two methods that an epidemic can be stamped out quickly. In the hands of good men, experience has taught that both these measures can be applied with scientific precision.

I recommend that both the screening and fumigation in cases of fever be carried out under the direct supervision of the medical officer of health and by his staff.

The staff of the medical officer should, without delay, be instructed how to seal a room, how to fumigate, and how to test the efficiency of the fumigation. The methods at present in vogue for fumigating and disinfecting for diphtheria, scarlet fever, etc., will not do.

A supply of the necessary materials for screening, including laths and frames, paper strips, fumigators, and fumigating material should be kept in the health office for emergency purposes, and the health officer should know where he can immediately procure additional supplies. Simple rules for the guidance of the men should be drawn up.

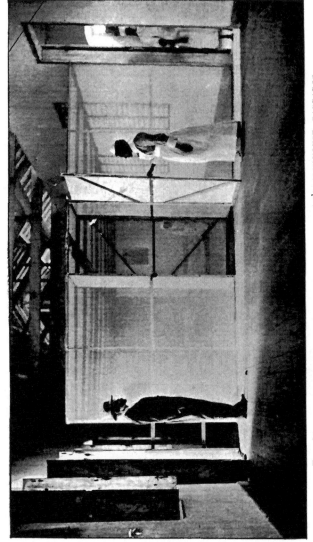

FIG. 25.—A TEMPORARY SCREENED WARD IN ST. LUCY'S ALMSHOUSE, BARBADOS.
Observe the double doors.

In my judgment, in view of the fact that mosquito-borne diseases cause more sickness and mortality in the tropics than those arising from any other cause, it is not too much to expect that sanitary inspectors and others attached to health offices in the tropics should be taught the precautions to take against them. This is, however, frequently omitted, and instead they are taught principles of European sanitation, which are inadequate to deal with malaria or yellow fever.

Screening the Patient and Room.—In either doubtful or well-marked cases the patient is to be at once placed under bars in charge of a nurse, and the room screened. The entrance to the room is to be through double doors (air-lock) provided for the purpose, the original door, if there was one, having been removed. The portable screens and doors used for the purpose may be made with wire gauze or bobinette, the standard gauge of eighteen meshes to the inch either way being used. Employing mosquito nets alone, or, as at Belize, portable screened chambers, is not sufficient—the presumption being that, as the majority of infected mosquitos are in the patient's room, it is essential that both their egress from the chamber and the entrance of fresh ones be prevented.

If screening cannot be carried out in the patient's room, or there is reason to believe that the double doors will be left open or the screens to the windows interfered with, then, without hesitation, the patient should be removed in the screened ambulance to the isolation hospital, otherwise the patient becomes a source of infection in the district.

II. To Exterminate the Carriers

Sealing and Fumigating.—Preparation for fumigation should have started with the screening. Not only the sick chamber, but very possibly also other rooms in the house harbour infected specimens of the stegomyia. The rule of procedure should, however, be absolute, and that is that the entire house must be fumigated, with the exception of the patient's room, which is screened.   Incomplete and imperfect fumigation are the principal reasons of not being able more promptly to suppress yellow fever.

Houses and huts in tropical countries have usually innumerable large and small openings in roof and sides, and it is contended that it would be difficult to seal them, or halls, stores, or markets without elaborate and expensive wooden framing.   As a matter of fact, and proved in numerous instances in tropical countries, an intelligent workman can, in an incredibly short time, paper over a whole archway, hall, or even court. By the use of a few supporting laths, and with stout and thin paper, the very large openings can be completely sealed.   The stout paper necessary for covering large openings can usually be procured locally and at once.   Paper cut in rolls, three inches wide, is exceedingly useful for pasting along the cracks, but it would be required to be ordered and to be kept in stock.   In an emergency, however, strips of newspaper could readily be cut.   Although it is recommended to seal the rooms from the inside, I think there is an advantage in sealing windows, etc., from the outside in order not

FIG. 26.—PAPER-SCREENING AN ARCHWAY PREVIOUS TO
FUMIGATION, NEW ORLEANS.

p. 140]

to disturb any mosquitos which may be present. If there are any fireplaces or other holes they will require to be sealed from the inside. The doorway is left open till the last to introduce the fumigating materials and to light up; when this has been done the door is brought to and sealed, and the time noted in a book kept for the purpose. The medical officer or the chief superintendent should personally examine to see that the sealing is carried out effectively. A small open chink admitting light is sufficient to attract mosquitos to it; then they make their escape. Halls, water-closets, or outhouses must not be forgotten.

Considerable objection amongst the poorer classes is usually taken to the disturbance of their homes and their displacement by the fumigation. *No excuse*, other than severe illness in a room, should be taken as exempting any part of the house from fumigation, except the sick room, which should be fumigated as soon as possible.

After the allotted time necessary to thoroughly complete the fumigation is up, the doors are opened and the floors swept. Some of the mosquitos may only be stupefied, and it is necessary that they be all burnt or otherwise destroyed.

After the patient is convalescent, or after death, the patient's room is to be fumigated.

Materials and Apparatus to be used in Fumigation, and precautions to be taken.—No guesses at the amount of material to be used are to be made, but the room should be carefully measured and materials proportioned to cubic capacity as follows (small closets and wardrobes to be opened):

Pyrethrum Powder.—3 lb. to 1,000 cubic ft. applied for three hours, and it is better that the 3 lb. be divided amongst three pots than that all the powder be put in one pot. The pots to be placed in pans containing a little water. Pyrethrum powder is used for rooms close to the sick patient, as the fumes which might escape from sulphur fumigation are irritating.

Pyrethrum powder is also used in cases where brass-work, pianos, telephones, instruments, etc., are present.

Sulphur.—2 lb. to 1,000 cubic ft. The pots containing the sulphur are to be placed in pans containing 1 in. of water. The sulphur is to be started by alcohol, and care must be taken to see that it is well alight. Duration, three hours. Brass-work and instruments are liable to injury ; they should, therefore, be removed.

Camphor and Carbolic Acid.—The mixture consists of equal parts camphor and crystallised carbolic acid dissolved by gentle heat. It is an exceedingly good fumigator, does not injure furniture, clothes, or brass-work ; the odour is pleasant and smells of camphor. A room has a refreshing smell after its use.

Four ounces are vaporised per 1,000 cubic ft. for two hours ; the material is placed in an open pan placed over a spirit or petroleum lamp, white vapour is given off. .

To test the efficiency of the fumigation, it is very useful to enclose some twenty or more mosquitos in a cigar or other small box covered on one side with

Fig. 28.

Fig. 27.

PAPERING OUTHOUSES PREVIOUS TO SULPHUR FUMIGATION, NEW ORLEANS.

muslin. The box is placed on the floor, and the mosquitos should be dead at the end of the fumigation. They should be kept, however, to see if they revive.

Avoid risk of setting fire to the premises by using care and foresight.

Fumigation of Adjacent Houses and General Fumigation.—It is most important that the houses in the vicinity of the house in which a case of yellow fever is declared should be fumigated at once. Powers are often sought by the authority to compel owners or occupiers of houses, building lots, outhouses, and premises situate within 100 yards of the infected house or premises, to destroy all mosquitos, larvæ, pupæ, etc. I am strongly of opinion that this is not sufficient. The householder cannot, as a rule, carry out fumigation as described above. It can only be carried out effectively by the proper staff, which should be that of the medical officer of health. The result of the householder carrying out fumigation is that the majority of the mosquitos are not killed, that cases of yellow fever occur in the so-called fumigated houses, and that the method is brought into disrepute. I do not think that the authorities always realise the necessity of issuing stringent directions for the destruction of the yellow fever mosquito. The following notice, for instance, is of little practical use:

" Inside of houses care should be taken to destroy mosquitos as much as possible, especially if there are any cases of fever in the neighbourhood. This may be done by burning either insect powder or tobacco leaf freely in the room after closing the doors and windows; afterwards sweeping the ceilings, walls, and floors, and destroying the sweepings (which will contain dead and stunned mosquitos) by fire."

This paragraph is of very little use to the householder, and it certainly will not bring about the effective destruction of mosquitos; on the contrary, a sense of false security may ensue. Those who have worked with culicides know that the quantities of materials to be used must be specified, the sealing must be complete, and the exposure a definite time; that a little practice is necessary, and that tobacco leaves are not used because it is exceedingly difficult to fire them, that special apparatus is necessary, and that the smell penetrates everything. I therefore recommend that the district authorities be given powers to execute fumigation in the houses surrounding the infected house, and that the distance be not specified, but that this be left to the discretion of the authority acting on the advice of the medical officer.

Whilst I am of opinion that the fumigation of an infected house and the houses surrounding should be carried out by the health authorities, I think that the inhabitants of the town should be encouraged to fumigate their houses in a systematic and scientific manner, and not to rely on carrying a little insect powder alight on a shovel through the rooms, which is as effective as the old native plan, still adopted in some places, of lighting bonfires in the streets. For that end I think that it would be of advantage if the

District Board would undertake for a nominal fee the fumigation of houses when they were applied to. If the camphor-carbolic compound is used, householders would be distinct gainers, as moths and objectionable vermin would be killed, and there would be no damage to furniture or clothes by either smell, smoke, smuts or corrosion.

CHAPTER XIII

THE *STEGOMYIA CALOPUS*

THIS mosquito, which has been conclusively demonstrated to be the sole transmitter of yellow fever, is a very characteristic and familiar one throughout the yellow fever zone. It is surmised, however, that it was originally imported into the Southern United States from the tropics through the medium of commercial intercourse. It is common on the coast towns along the Gulf, the Caribbean Sea, and on the Atlantic coast of tropical and subtropical countries. It is, therefore, a mosquito of the seaports, and this is one of the reasons why it is so essential to eradicate it, especially in view of the continual opening of new ports throughout the tropics. It is capable of flourishing over a wide area, and Dr. Howard of Washington states from collected observations that the species can flourish wherever the sum of the mean daily temperature above 6° C. (43° F.) throughout the year does not fall below 10,000° C. It is not by any means exclusively confined to the coast line, observations

FIG. 29.—A ROW OF WATER-BARRELS AND KEROSENE TINS, TYPICAL BREEDING PLACES OF THE STEGOMYIA, BELIZE.

p. 146]

showing that in places where it is capable of surviving the winter it readily spreads into the interior, following the trade routes, whether rail or river. It has already, it is stated, reached an altitude of 4,200 feet in Mexico (yellow fever working party Report), and, as shown by the great outbreak of yellow fever in the interior of Guatemala and Spanish Honduras in 1905, it has well established itself along the Puerto Barrios and Puerto Cortez railroads.

It is essentially a domestic mosquito, and, therefore, a mosquito of cities. Whilst the malaria-bearing Anophelines are usually confined to the outskirts of large cities, having been gradually driven away from the centre of the towns owing to the building up of inhabited blocks, and to drainage, the stegomyia, on the contrary, seeks the central and more crowded parts of the city—the places, in fact, where it finds the necessary and innumerable water receptacles in the closest proximity to the dwelling houses. The knowledge of this characteristic is of the utmost importance in all epidemics. It is, indeed, a cistern-breeding mosquito, and is often known on this account as the " cistern mosquito." It is found in abundance, therefore, in those places where rain-water is collected and stored for domestic purposes; no wonder, then, that it was present in New Orleans, with its sixty to seventy thousand water-vats.

The mosquito is readily recognised by the white bands upon the legs and abdomen, the lyre-shaped pattern in white on the back of the thorax. It is due to the presence of these bands and spots that this black-and-white mosquito is often called the "Tiger Mosquito." The females only suck blood, and they appear to attack man both during the day and at night. Between 4 p.m. and midnight is stated by some to be their most active period. For this reason it is necessary to take precautions against them at night as well as by day. The stegomyia is subject to seasonal variations, cold being the great factor in stopping biting activity and breeding. Below 75° F. development is retarded, and the eggs kept at a temperature of 68° F. do not hatch. It is for this reason that the onset of cold weather in New Orleans soon put an end to yellow fever, and that the city is said to enjoy a natural immunity from December to May. Too much stress must not be laid upon this, however, as the fact remains that the mosquito readily survives through the winter. The distribution and history of this mosquito in towns during these months require close investigation. Each female lays between twenty and seventy-five eggs on the surface of the water ; these are minute, black, and cigar-shaped ; they are very resistant, and have been kept in a dry state for periods varying between ten and twenty days, and freezing does not destroy their fertility. The eggs are therefore a ready means of tiding over the cold weather. Under suitable conditions of temperature the eggs hatch out, according to different observers, in from ten hours to three days. The result is the well-known " wiggle waggle," or " wiggle tails," the larval stage of the mosquito. The larvæ are very active and very sensitive, and very rapidly disappear

FIG. 30.—A COOLIE "RANGE," SHOWING THE WATER-BARRELS; THEY ARE ALL SCREENED. SUGAR PLANTATION DIAMOND, DEMERARA.

p. 148]

from the surface of the water in the cistern if the least disturbance occurs. For this reason the water barrel or vat must be approached gently if one is desirous of obtaining specimens and examining them, otherwise they wriggle very rapidly to the bottom. Another point has also to be borne in mind, and that is, that they cling to the sides of the receptacle and hide in the crevices, so that it is by no means easy to get rid of them. Simply emptying the water out of the receptacle will not suffice ; a very thorough rinsing and cleansing is necessary. The duration of the larval period is from six and a half to eight days normally ; but, of course, they may remain in the larval stage for a much longer period ; for instance, I brought some specimens alive to Liverpool which I collected at Puerto Barrios in Guatemala, on October 26. They were kept in a large test-tube either in my pocket or in my living room, and they were exposed to great variations of temperature, the cold increasing as I travelled from New Orleans to New York, and from New York across the Atlantic to Liverpool. The journey occupied twenty-five days, and they were only supplied with clean water. The larval stage is succeeded by the pupa stage, which lasts two days or under, and from the pupa arises the image or winged mosquito.

Dr. Francis of the United States Marine Hospital Service reported, on March 25, 1907, upon many interesting points in connection with the life cycle of *Stegomyia calopus*, as observed in Mobile. Amongst them he mentions that larvæ were never found breeding in the unpaved street gutters or ponds, or in fact in any natural earth-bottoms, but were always in artificial water-containers.   The eggs may retain their vitality when kept dry for six and a half months.   In my experience in searching for stegomyia larvæ—and it is now considerable—I have invariably found the rain-water barrel the seat of election for breeding purposes. Given an old wooden barrel, just coated with a green slime, and "worms" will almost invariably be found. So expert did my men become in detecting likely breeding places that they frequently affirmed that worms must be in a barrel from its appearance ; yet a cursory examination of the water failed to reveal their presence.   When, however, the water was poured out to all but a teacupful at the bottom, and this was well agitated, invariably the worms were found.   This property of disappearing to the bottom of the recep-tacle and hiding in the chinks between the staves and in the groove at the bottom is very characteristic. After barrels come washing-tubs, olive jars, and then every form of water receptacle.   I have found them in the blacksmith's shop in his cooling barrel or tank, and in logs.   It can be stated that, wherever in or around a house water stagnates, there the larvæ will be found.   Their presence is a positive test of stagnant water.   In the living and bed rooms they are frequently found in receptacles for holding flowers, and in which the water is imperfectly removed ; very frequently, indeed, in vessels in which a cutting of a croton plant is placed in order to make it take root.   In my opinion the essential point is that the stagnant water be in or

around the house—that is, in the yard or garden. One
does not encounter them breeding, at any rate in
large numbers, away from man ; they are as domestic
as the flea, bug, and cat. In a few instances I have
found them in drains in the houses, mixed with *culex*
larvæ. In these cases the water was dirty. This latter
point recalls the statement often made that larvæ purify
water, and that they are useful in the drinking-water
butts because they will remove pathogenic organisms
should any gain access. For this reason certain
municipal authorities have not been so active in their
destruction as they might otherwise have been. We
have no evidence whatever that they do remove
pathogenic germs ; their natural food is green algæ
and diatoms. But from the practical point of view,
we know the danger of stegomyia larvæ and how surely
yellow fever will spread wherever these larvæ are, that
it is hardly practical to keep these larvæ for any supposed good they may do when we know the positive
disaster they bring about.

Stegomyia Survey.—In every town I have visited
for the purpose of strengthening or drawing up
measures against fellow fever, it has been my invariable
rule to visit either all the houses or to take representative blocks, and go through each house, garden,
and yard systematically. In these tours I am accompanied by the sanitary inspectors and one or more
medical officers. We are armed with white enamelled
iron spoons, with which we can rapidly take a sample
of water and see if larvæ are present. I examined
all water, drinking and washing, inside or outside the

house, and whether contained in cisterns, barrels, buckets, tubs, tins, goblets, vases, " monkeys," " destilladores," wells, antiformicas, broken bottles, etc. If larvæ are found for the first time, the householder is handed a printed slip setting forth the danger of having larvæ, and the penalty for the same. If after previous warning they are found, the householder is summoned.

In the West Indian Islands the percentage of stegomyia breeding places in the towns and large villages has varied from 4 to 10 per cent. Our aim is to reduce it to zero.

NOTE —The stegomyia is often described as the mosquito of seaports, but it must always be remembered that it is by no means limited to them. It is simply more abundant in seaports, because there are more people crowded together there ; but let the labourers of the population migrate into the mountains with their paraphernalia and innumerable receptacles for holding water, and stegomyia will go as certainly as do the flea, the dog, the cat, and all the other domestic animals and insects which follow man along his paths, be they by rail or over sea.

CHAPTER XIV

THE YELLOW FEVER CAMPAIGNS IN (1) HAVANA, CUBA;
(2) NEW ORLEANS; (3) HONDURAS; (4) RIO; SANTOS;
(5) CANAL ZONE; (6) WEST INDIES; AMAZON

THE ANTI-YELLOW FEVER CAMPAIGN IN HAVANA, 1900

THIS will always remain one of the first and one of the greatest examples of what has been done to stamp out a disease by concerted intelligent action and using the latest and most modern weapons. When the American Government took over the administration of Cuba, one of the first things to be done was to make Havana a livable place. Hitherto it had been a notoriously unhealthy place, the natural home of most pestilences, and with a corresponding mortality. Thus we know that between the years 1853–1900 there perished in the city of Havana alone 35,952 persons of yellow fever. This is equivalent to 754 a year, 64 a month, or to 2 deaths a day. And now, after General Woods, Colonel Gorgas, Guiteras, Finlay and their other distinguished colleagues, to whom we have had occasion to refer, took the situation firmly in hand and organised a thoroughly efficient sanitary administration and a special raid upon the breeding places of the stegomyia, the death rate for Cuba has come down to between 11–17 pro mille! It must never be forgotten that it was in Cuba that the crucial and famous test was made that only by the stegomyia could the poison of yellow fever be transmitted. This test was made, as we have already seen in a preceding chapter, by Reed, Carroll, Agramonte, and Lazear. Yellow fever has now been checked and annihilated. Thus in 1907 only one case of yellow fever is reported in Havana, and the general death rate is 17 pro mille. It can be with truth said to-day, as stated in the current number of the "Bulletin of Public Health and Charities of Cuba," that during the three years between 1905–9 there was only a total of 359 cases of yellow fever throughout the whole republic, and during that same period only 40 deaths in Havana; whereas in the days of old there were thousands of cases.

On the date upon which this new Bulletin was issued (April of this year), the republic was declared free from small-pox, yellow fever, and bubonic plague. This is the result of the use of modern weapons—a complete triumph for civilisation.

THE YELLOW FEVER CAMPAIGN, NEW ORLEANS, 1905

This having been my first campaign in which I was present as a volunteer, I will trace the steps by which the fever was overcome, for that purpose reproducing the proclamations which were issued in their chrono-

logical order. They will always act as a guide in the
case of a yellow fever outbreak. New Orleans at the
time had an estimated population of 325,000 of mixed
nationalities. There was a large Italian and Sicilian
labour population housed in the oldest and dirtiest part
of the town, and amongst them yellow fever broke out.
It was clear that before the citizens recognised that
they had yellow fever in their city, that disease had
gained a firm foothold unperceived. Then, when the
seriousness of the situation was realised, the first step
was to organise the resources of the city to combat the
disease, and the following manifesto was issued by the
Health Authority and Advisory Committee.

Step 1

An emergency exists in our city to-day which
demands the attention of every individual, with the
view to limiting and preventing the spread of epidemic
disease. It has been scientifically proved that the
mosquito is the only means of the transmission of
yellow fever, and measures should be especially directed
against them. It is especially urged by the undersigned
that the following simple directions be followed by the
householders of this city for the summer months :—

1. Empty all unused receptacles of water. Allow
no stagnant water on the premises.

2. Screen cisterns, after placing a small quantity of
insurance oil (a teacupful in each cistern) on the surface
of the water.

3. Place a small quantity of insurance oil in cesspools or privy vaults.

4. Sleep under mosquito nets.

5. Screen doors and windows wherever possible with fine screen wire.

Step 2.—APPEAL FOR CIVIC CO-OPERATION

On Monday, July 24, a Proclamation was issued, signed by the Mayor, and concurred in by the Medical Authorities, setting forth the situation and calling upon the citizens to co-operate with the Health Authorities in stamping out the fever. It runs as follows ;—

THE MOSQUITO CAMPAIGN

PROCLAMATION

MAYORALTY OF NEW ORLEANS,
CITY HALL, *July* 24, 1905

TO THE PEOPLE OF NEW ORLEANS :—

The health situation in this city is serious, but not alarming. Because of this situation, quarantine has been declared against New Orleans by several States and Cities. It is proper that the actual facts be recognised and dealt with resolutely and calmly.

It is authoritatively stated by eminent sanitarians that within recent years visitations of yellow fever, more widely spread than that which is in our city, have been successfully met and absolutely suppressed by methods whose potency has been demonstrated by ascertained results, and the application of which is simple. Those methods are now adopted by our own State and City Health Authorities, with the volunteer assistance of the United States Marine Hospital Service, and the Orleans Parish Medical Society of this parish. To the perfect and speedy success of the measures to be followed, the co-operation of every householder is necessary. That given, the people may confidently expect a speedy release from the trying conditions in which they are now placed, and from apprehension of its recurrence in the future.

I, therefore, as Mayor, urge all citizens and householders to render cordial and ready obedience to the instructions which may from time to time be given by the Health Authorities, and to render every aid within their power to those Authorities in the earnest efforts which they are now making, and in which they will persist for the absolute stamping out of this infection. Those instructions are not difficult of performance; they are easily to be understood, and can be followed with but little expense. Since the consensus of sanitary and medical opinion of to-day is that the infection of yellow fever is transmitted, or can be transmitted, only by means of the sting of the insect known as the "cistern mosquito," the following advice recently given by Dr. Kohnke, the City's Health Officer; by Dr. Souchon, President of the State Board of Health; Dr. White, Surgeon of the U.S. Marine Hospital Service, and an Advisory Committee of the Orleans Parish Medical Society, should be willingly and implicitly obeyed by every householder in this city.

1. To keep empty all unused receptacles of water in every house, and allow no stagnant water on any premises.

2. To screen all cisterns after placing a small quantity of insurance oil (a teacupful in each cistern) on the surface of the water.

3. To place a small quantity of insurance oil in cesspools or privy vaults.

4. Sleep under mosquito nets.

5. Wherever practicable, screen doors and windows with wire screens of close mesh.

The foregoing advice may from time to time be given by the Health Authorities with more particularity. Whatever emanates from them must be accepted as given for the good of the city and the preservation of every individual of its population, and should be respected and followed to the letter.

I repeat, upon the information of those qualified from actual investigation and scientific knowledge to speak upon this subject, that the situation in our city is not alarming, and that if it is treated by our people earnestly and intelligently, that this situation will soon be eliminated and demonstration will be made to the world that for the future the infection of yellow fever can have no permanent lodgment within the borders of the City of New Orleans.

Step 3.—APPEAL FOR EARLY NOTIFICATION

ISSUED BY THE HEALTH AUTHORITIES AND ADVISORY COMMITTEE

July 24, 1905

Dear Doctor,

We want to specially urge you to report all your cases of fever—malarial, typhoid fever or fever of any kind—during this summer, to the City Board of Health. It is absolutely essential to the checking of the spread of yellow fever in our city that all cases of fever should be promptly and conscientiously reported. Our patients, the public and the surrounding communities, will naturally look to our profession in this great emergency, and the responsibility rests in a great measure with us to check this condition, or at least to limit its too extensive spread. It is a well-known and scientifically proven dogma that the mosquito theory is to be accepted as a fact ; then we must exert ourselves to the utmost to destroy the mosquito, the only host of transmission of yellow fever. Let us, then, make a consistent campaign against it, educate our patients regarding this situation and the danger of it, and direct them to place patients immediately under netting pending action of the Board of Health. Neither your patient nor the household will be subjected to the obnoxious house quarantine of several years ago.

Above all things, *report your cases promptly*, to permit us to check any further foci of infection.

Even if you are not positive that the mosquito is the only source of transmission of yellow fever, give your city the benefit of the doubt in this important and vital matter.

Step 4.—APPEAL FOR IMMEDIATE SCREENING OF ALL SUSPICIOUS CASES AND FOR FUMIGATION

ISSUED BY THE ADVISORY COMMITTEE

ORLEANS PARISH MEDICAL SOCIETY,
NEW ORLEANS, LA.

DEAR DOCTOR,
In an earnest attempt to work in harmony with the plan of procedure adopted by the Health Authority and the U.S. Public Health and Marine Hospital Service, now being enforced in a general inspection of our entire city, we want to suggest to you, as your Advisory Committee acting with these bodies, that you report at once any case of fever in your practice remotely suspicious of being yellow fever. If you want to do your city the greatest good in this hour of trial, immediately constitute yourself as a Health Officer for the premises of the sick you are called to

attend. Even before the regular Sanitary Inspector of the Board reaches the house, place the patient at once under a mosquito bar, pending further proceedings. Also order at once another room fumigated with sulphur—2 lb. to the 1,000 cubic feet—and then thoroughly screen it. If it cannot be done in a perfect manner, at least order all the openings screened with either cheese cloth or other light material, well packed so as to allow no mosquitos in the room. Keep only one door free, covering all the transoms in the same manner. On entering the door beat the air thoroughly with a cloth before opening. When the room is prepared, remove the patient to it, fumigating the room just vacated in the same manner.

After the first three days of the fever the *Stegomyia fasciata* cannot be infected from that patient, but we must be careful to keep the room well closed until the final fumigation or destruction of any mosquitos which might have remained in the room. Look to the general hygiene of the house, inquire whether the cisterns or any other open receptacles of standing water about the premises have been properly oiled or screened. Act in this manner regardless of the work which will be done by the constituted authorities, for your own personal good and for the greatest good of your city. In other words, Doctor, take every possible precaution to protect all of your fever cases from being bitten by mosquitos during the first three days of fever.

Our interest in this entire matter is the same as yours, and we must work for the same purpose. The part to be played by our profession is an extremely important one; the faith and trust of the entire community is placed on our shoulders, and we must fully deserve the confidence reposed in us.

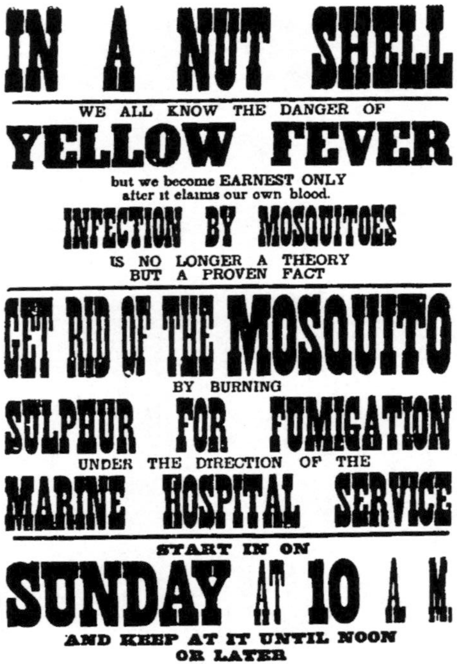

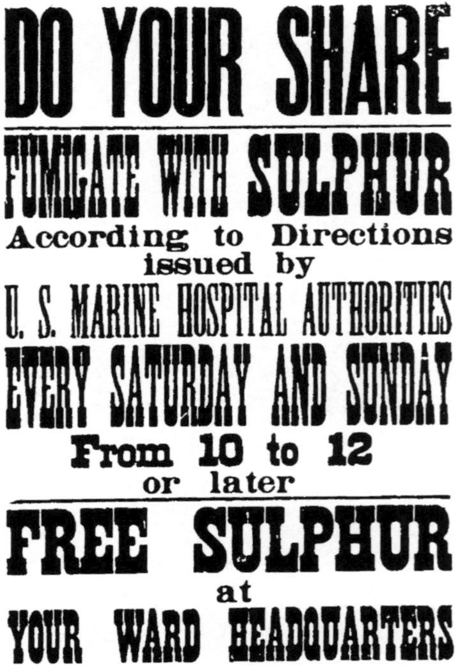

DO YOUR SHARE

FUMIGATE WITH SULPHUR

According to Directions
issued by

U. S. MARINE HOSPITAL AUTHORITIES

EVERY SATURDAY AND SUNDAY

From 10 to 12
or later

FREE SULPHUR

at

YOUR WARD HEADQUARTERS

Fig. 32

IN A NUT SHELL

WE ALL KNOW THE DANGER OF

YELLOW FEVER

but we become EARNEST ONLY
after it claims our own blood.

INFECTION BY MOSQUITOES

IS NO LONGER A THEORY
BUT A PROVEN FACT

GET RID OF THE MOSQUITO

BY BURNING

SULPHUR FOR FUMIGATION

UNDER THE DIRECTION OF THE

MARINE HOSPITAL SERVICE

START IN ON

SUNDAY AT 10 A. M.

AND KEEP AT IT UNTIL NOON
OR LATER

Fig. 31.

EXAMPLES OF POSTERS DURING NEW ORLEANS YELLOW FEVER EPIDEMIC, 1905

Step 5.—APPEAL FOR AN EDUCATIONAL CAMPAIGN

ISSUED BY THE ADVISORY COMMITTEE

Another circular is issued on the 24th, directed to the Board of Health, pointing out the necessity of a campaign of education, and urging the importance of asking the clergy to especially disseminate knowledge from the pulpit in the matter of yellow fever. The circular then proceeds to give useful information in case of infection and finally appeals for united action in a general warfare against the stegomyia.

New Orleans,
July 24, 1905

Gentlemen,

The condition existing at present is one that calls for the most strenuous, prompt and vigorous measures capable of institution. In view of the absence of the necessity for obnoxious local or house quarantine, the co-operation of physician and householder should be a matter of comparatively easy solution. A campaign of education should be boldly inaugurated. The clergyman, during his rounds and from his pulpit, should be a valuable agent in the dissemination of this knowledge. The Advisory Committee of the Orleans Parish Medical Society begs to recommend that the following measures be instituted at once, with the view of stamping out the few foci of infection of yellow fever which now exist in our city.

Cases of fever of any character developing in the infected area may be regarded as suspicious, and the patient immediately protected from mosquitos. The house, cisterns, yards, drains, gutters, cesspools and

11

vaults should be carefully inspected, and no breeding spots for mosquitos should be overlooked.

The gutters and streets must not be neglected.

If the case proves to be one of yellow fever, the house must be screened and the rooms in the house other than the one occupied by the patient must be fumigated, to destroy all mosquitos in them.   When the case ends, either by recovery or death, the room occupied by the patient must be fumigated, for the same reason.

The success of these procedures will largely depend upon the promptness and earnestness with which mosquitos are prevented from coming in contact with the patient and the destruction of all mosquitos in the room after the patient is cured or dies.

The new foci of infection must be diligently sought and drastic measures adopted for stamping them out. It is only through the proper conciliatory education of the physician and the layman, and through their sincere co-operation, that anything can be accomplished.

For the vast portion of the city not infected, we recommend that a sufficiently large force of men be immediately organised to place oil in all unscreened cisterns, or other breeding places of mosquitos, and distribute circulars amongst householders enlisting their co-operation.

All gutters should either be flushed or oiled.

An active, vigorous and persistent warfare on mosquitos should, in our opinion, be immediately instituted from one end of the city to the other, as in this way localities now healthy may be kept so, even though foci of infection be introduced.   We believe that the sanitary regeneration of this city depends entirely upon prompt and vigorous action on your part.

With the profoundest assurance of our heartiest co-operation with you in any movement to better the sanitary conditions of the city.

Step 6.—A WARNING TO BEWARE OF THE DANGER OF OVERLOOKING THE LESS OBVIOUS BREEDING PLACES OF THE STEGOMYIA

A very useful and practical notice is also sent out by the Advisory Committee directing attention to the importance of not overlooking possible receptacles of water in the house, as pitchers, flower-pots, etc. It reads as follows :—

ORLEANS PARISH MEDICAL SOCIETY,
NEW ORLEANS, LA.

We desire to call your special attention to the wrigglers seen inside of the residences of people. Probably the public in the fight against the mosquito have directed all their efforts against the cisterns and the barrels or the outside containers. Still a source of great danger also exists inside of the bedrooms in the water-pitchers, in the dining-room, or in the conservatory in the water-pots, vases or pots of plants. A frequent error and a great menace is the habit which some householders have of only partly emptying a water-pitcher, and though it is refilled daily it is never emptied entirely, leaving always one-half pint or so for the larvæ to develop. Any physician in his daily rounds can see this illustrated by inspecting the various water-pitchers in the bedrooms.

On this same line we beg to again call your attention to the accumulation of water in the urns in the cemeteries as well as in the sagged gutters of the house drains, which are a great source of mosquito breeding after rain.

Step 7.—APPEAL FOR A MORE SKILLED MEDICAL
BODY TO CONDUCT THE CAMPAIGN

On August 4, the fever still making headway in
spite of all local efforts, the Advisory Board takes
very decided action. It candidly expresses the opinion
that it has not confidence in the efficacy of the work
performed up to date ; *that this work must be absolutely
perfect in its working to be efficient,* and that to accomplish the desired reorganisation it is necessary to call
in the assistance of the Public Health and Marine
Hospital Service of the United States.

NEW ORLEANS,
August 4, 1905

CITY BOARD OF HEALTH.

GENTLEMEN,

As there has appeared a new case in the
Frye focus, which has been in existence since Monday,
while we had been told that the instructions previously
agreed upon in the management of all maturing foci
had been rigidly carried out, and especially so in this
case. As we are not satisfied that the fumigation
performed by the City Board of Health has been
absolutely effective, we feel, as we have shared some
of the responsibility of this work, that it is a matter
of too great importance to be kept on in this unorganised
and unsystematic manner. This is the first serious
visitation of yellow fever in this country since the
mosquito has been recognised as the only mode of
transmission, and we are unwilling to support the
City Board of Health in what we consider an ineffective
service.

Step 8.—LETTER WARNING MEDICAL MEN NOT TO
OVERLOOK THE MILD TYPE OF YELLOW FEVER
WHICH MAY BE FOUND IN THE NATIVE BORN

NEW ORLEANS, LA.,
August 17, 1905

DEAR DOCTOR,

In the consistent campaign we are now waging
throughout the city against the fever, we want to enlist
your hearty assistance.

You have shown up to now a uniform activity, and
if some of the work already accomplished begins to
show some little improvement, we feel it is greatly
due to your co-operation. This, though, is a crucial
moment, and you must keep up reporting all your cases
with unfailing promptness. *The native born will undoubtedly begin to be affected, and will show the lightest
and mildest types of the disease; it is specially with
regard to these that we wish to warn you, for it is as
important to the success of the work being done by the
U.S.P.H. and Marine Hospital Service, that the mild
cases be reported as well as the marked cases. These
must be screened as carefully as others.*

One stegomyia infected, in the first three days from
such a case, can produce a number of serious and even
fatal cases. The means employed are being systematised
and rendered less objectionable daily by the service, so
let us endure a little inconvenience for the welfare
of all.

Beware of the so-called immunisation or acclimatisation fever, and report these cases as promptly and
rigidly as if they were perfectly characteristic, so that
the authorities will be able to give them the same
SANITARY TREATMENT.

Step 9.—APPEAL TO HOUSEHOLDERS TO DELAY "MOVING DAY" ON ACCOUNT OF DANGER OF SPREADING INFECTION

In view of the near approach of "Moving Day" (October 1) the undersigned deem it their duty to direct your attention to the danger likely to attend a general moving of tenants from house to house.

Persons moving from infected localities may later develop the fever in uninfected neighbourhoods, thereby developing new foci. Others now residing in uninfected houses may contract the disease by removing into houses where mild cases of fever may have occurred and recovered without medical attention, and consequently escaping fumigation. Non-immunes coming into such houses will almost inevitably contract yellow fever, thereby adding to our present troubles.

We do therefore urge the importance of taking such steps as may be necessary to delay the general movement for at least thirty days.

ADVISORY COMMITTEE, O.P.M.S.

Step 10.—DANGER OF REMOVAL OF TEMPORARY CISTERN SCREENS

NEW ORLEANS, LA.,
September 13, 1905

There being a pretty general understanding in the community that the cheese-cloth screens over cisterns have to be removed by October 1, and the regular 18-mesh to the inch wire screen substituted by that date, we believe that a number of persons are now having this change done to the great danger of a general liberation of all mosquitos imprisoned or bred from the pupæ in the cisterns. We cannot afford, in

FIG. 34.—SCREENING GANG AT WORK. SCREENING THE
WATER CISTERNS. NEW ORLEANS, 1905.

FIG. 33.—AN OILING AND CISTERN-SCREENING GANG.
NEW ORLEANS, 1905.

the final fight of checking yellow fever in our midst, to neglect so important a matter as this, so we strongly urge that the change from cheese cloth to wire, if not legally postponed until Dec. 1, shall be by having the wire screens placed over the cheese cloth without removing the latter.

ADVISORY COMMITTEE, O.P.M.S.

Public opinion having been educated, the City Authority feels now strong enough to bring in an ordinance to compel landlords to screen all vats.

Step 11.—A WATER-CISTERN SCREENING ORDINANCE

MAYORALTY OF NEW ORLEANS,
CITY HALL, *August* 2, 1905

NO. 3196 NEW COUNCIL SERIES

AN ORDINANCE, prescribing the manner in which water liable to breed mosquitos shall be stored within the limits of the City of New Orleans.

Section 1.—Be it ordained by the Council of the City of New Orleans that no water liable to breed mosquitos shall be stored within the limits of the city, except under the following conditions.

Section 2.—Water kept in cisterns, tanks, barrels, buckets, or other containers for a period longer than one week shall be protected from mosquitos in the following manner : Cisterns shall be covered with oil by the property owner or agent thereof within forty-eight hours after the promulgation of this ordinance and provided with a cover of wood or metal ; all openings in the top or within 6 ft. of the top larger than $\frac{1}{16}$ in. to be screened with netting of not less than 18-mesh, or cheese cloth or other suitable material by the property owner or agent thereof within forty-eight hours after the promulgation of this ordinance, provided that after the first day of October 1905, all property owners shall be required to screen cisterns with wire netting of the proper size mesh as required by the Board of Health in such a manner as to prevent the entrance of mosquitos.

Section 3.—Tanks or barrels or similar containers to be constructed in the manner provided for cisterns, or in some other manner satisfactory to the Board of Health.

Section 4.—Buckets containing water for longer than one week (such as fire buckets in cotton presses), and other similar containers of stagnant water, shall be covered in such a manner as to prevent the entrance of mosquitos.

Section 5.—Water in ponds, pools, or basins, in public or private parks, places of resort or residence, or in depressions, or excavations made for any purpose, shall be stocked with mosquito-destroying fish, or covered with protective netting, or shall be drained off at least once every week, or shall be covered with coal oil in a manner satisfactory to the Board of Health, by the owner or agent thereof within forty-eight hours after the promulgation of this ordinance.

Section 6.—The Board of Health may, in its discretion whenever deemed necessary, treat stagnant water by applying oil to its surface in such a manner as to destroy mosquitos.

Section 7.—The penalty for violations of this ordinance or any section thereof shall be a fine of not more than twenty-five dollars, or imprisonment for not more than thirty days, or both, and failure to comply with any provision shall be considered a separate offence for each day of its continuance after the proper notification by the Board of Health.

Adopted by the Council of the City of New Orleans.

Step 12.—A DAY APPOINTED TO "CLEAN UP" IN THE CITY

The following is an appeal to the citizens to "clean up," and it again should be copied by all towns in the Yellow Fever zone.

THE MAYOR'S PROCLAMATION

It has come to be recognised as an indispensable necessity for the eradication of disease, and for the proper safeguarding of our public health, that our city should be thoroughly cleaned. Our patriotic citizens are unanimous in the sentiment and have generously come forward to aid and assist in such a movement.

The Executive Committee which was named to consider and take action upon the thorough cleansing of the city, recommended that Wednesday, August 9, 1905, be observed as general cleaning-up day. To that end, and to promote the more expeditious handling of the accumulations of dirt, it has been recommended that all householders begin the work of cleaning their premises Monday, and continue the same Tuesday, in order that the refuse and pilings will be ready and convenient for removal Wednesday, "General Cleaning-up Day."

It has been earnestly and urgently recommended that all merchants and business men assist in this work by closing their respective establishments on that day, so that they and their employees may assist in the .task.   There have been many patriotic offers of carts, wagons, teams and drays, and all contractors who are engaged in work of public improvement are urged to contribute their teams to aid in this laudable undertaking of removing trash and pilings. The details of this work will be planned and prepared under the direction and control of the Commissioner of Public Works, to whom the tender of carts, teams, etc., must be made as soon as possible in order that the full programme may be perfected and made public not later than Tuesday morning.

In furtherance of this great object, I do hereby call upon every taxpayer and householder to extend every assistance towards the effective performance of the work, and urging that all merchants and business men close their respective establishments on that day, I do hereby proclaim Wednesday, August 9, 1905, to be "General Cleaning-up Day."

Witness my hand and seal of office, affixed this fourth day of August, A.D. 1905.

MARTIN BEHRMAN,
Mayor.

Step 13.—APPEAL TO THE CLERGY
FROM THE CITIZENS' VOLUNTEER WARD ORGANISATION

NEW ORLEANS, LA.,
July 29, 1905

TO THE REVEREND CLERGY :

The influence of the Reverend Clergy is such, and their loyalty and public spirit have been so often demonstrated, that we venture to ask your co-operation with the Citizens' Volunteer Organisations in the present emergency.

United action produces the surest results.

We beg to ask that you will speak to your congregations on Sunday, July 30, or at the earliest date thereafter convenient to yourself, in behalf of the work now being carried on by the Health Authorities of the city.

We ask that you will urge them, whether they believe in the "mosquito theory" or not, that they will give their hearty assistance to the authorities who are attempting to stamp out the mosquito, as at least one source of infection. Urge upon them the patriotic duty of allowing cisterns to be oiled and screened; cesspools to be treated with disinfectants, etc.

Many householders (a small minority, but still enough to work mischief) refuse permission to the oilers and screeners to do the work. This refusal nullifies to a great extent the work accomplished on the premises of willing householders. In previous visitations of the fever we have been fighting in the dark, striking at an unknown enemy coming from a mysterious source.

The consensus of scientific opinion fixes upon the mosquito as the agent of transmission of the Yellow Fever.

The enemy therefore is in sight. So far as your power extends, then, we beg of you to use it for the spread of information concerning the mosquito theory, and to use your influence with your congregations to hold up the hands of the constituted Health Authorities.

This office will gladly receive suggestions and will give all possible assistance to the Ward Organisations.

It is proposed to have two cleaning-up days, by proclamation of the Mayor, although this has not at this writing been definitely decided.

The daily newspapers will announce it when determined. We will ask you to bring this matter also to the attention of your congregations.

Step 14.—REQUEST TO THE HOUSEHOLDERS OF
THE WARD TO OBSERVE A GENERAL
FUMIGATION DAY

NEW ORLEANS, LA.,
September 1, 1905

Saturday, September 2, and Sunday, September 3, have been suggested and agreed upon as GENERAL FUMIGATION DAYS, between the hours of 10 a.m. and 12 a.m., for the purpose of destroying mosquitos, which are recognised as the medium of communication of yellow fever, and we make the following suggestions as to the manner of fumigating :—

1.   Close all outside openings, such as doors and windows, and make the house (or room) to be fumigated as tight as possible, by closing or stopping the fireplace and other openings with paper pasted over them.

2.   Pianos should be removed from the rooms to be fumigated.

3.   Place an iron vessel, flat skillet preferred, in pan or tub with about one inch of water in it ; place roll of sulphur or flower of sulphur (two pounds to each ordinary-sized room to be fumigated) in the skillet ; pour over it a small quantity of alcohol, about two tablespoonfuls to the pound, and set fire to same.

4.   Keep the house, or rooms, closed for two hours after lighting the sulphur.

Those who prefer to do so may use pyrethrum powder (insect powder) instead of sulphur. Where this is used the rooms should be swept after the fumigation and the mosquitos so gathered up should be burned, as pyrethrum powder merely stuns the mosquito. The amount of pyrethrum to be used is one pound to each ordinary-sized room.

It having been decided to call in experts to advise upon the situation and if possible to expedite the campaign, the special yellow fever experts arrived and took charge of the situation, and the campaign was carried out with renewed energy and precision. It consisted in :—

1. Discovering every case of yellow fever and isolating it.

2. Killing all stegomyias.

3. General warfare against all mosquitos, except swamp.

4. Ensuring that each Ward was fully equipped with its forces of inspectors, oilers, screeners, fumigators and others as wanted, and that there was an adequate number of men.

Each Ward Office was in telephonic communication with the Central Office.

Under the Marine Hospital Surgeon in each Ward were placed one or more medical assistants, young local medical men, chosen on account of their local knowledge and ability, and a staff of workmen, varying from 28 to 128.

Each Ward Centre was furnished with a supply of—

Fumigating Materials.—Sulphur, pyrethrum, pots

for fumigating, paper, paste, laths and all accessories for sealing.

Screening Materials.—Bobinette and sheeting, wire, portable wire-screened doors, ladders, nails, hammers and all accessories.

Oiling Materials.—Oil and oil cans, ladders, scythes for cutting rank grass, carts.

A map of the district was kept at each office and the progress of the cases, the number of cisterns oiled, and of houses fumigated were recorded with dates. The various gangs, whether inspectors, oilers, screeners or fumigators, left the Ward Offices early in the morning for their appointed tasks, or at such time as they were particularly required. A practitioner might report a case to the Central Office or directly to the Ward Office in which the case occurred. If in the former manner, the Central Office telephoned to the Ward Officer concerned. As the result of the call, a screening and fumigating gang (see illustration) would be dispatched, the patient's room would be screened and the rest of the house fumigated, or the patient would be removed in the ambulance (see illustration) to the Emergency Hospital, and the house fumigated. Depending upon circumstances, the surrounding blocks would also be fumigated, and from the tenth to the thirtieth day of the occurrence of the case the Medical Inspector would visit the house every day to locate any secondary cases.

The work of the Central Office consisted in directing the work of the Wards, receiving reports of cases, preparing and issuing reports and instructions, and in generally organising. For these purposes a large clerical staff, as well as a statistical department and accountants' office, were necessary. All cases of fever had to be notified to this office, and it was in constant receipt of innumerable complaints and questions. Every morning either Dr. White or Dr. Richardson made an inspection tour of the districts. It was soon found necessary, in order to check unnecessary expenditure, to establish a *purveyor's office*. This was placed in the charge of Dr. Perkins and a staff of about twelve assistants. Each Ward was required to send in a requisition to this department for the material it wanted, which, if not in stock, was promptly obtained. In this way waste was avoided, and by purchasing supplies beforehand in the cheapest markets, considerable saving was effected. The office was most carefully organised and everything was reduced to a very precise system.

Total Number Employed in the Campaign

Total number of men, inspectors, oilers,
    screeners, etc.. 910
Special Fumigating Division . . 156
Special Investigating Division . . 105
Purveyor's Department . . . 32
                                  1,203

The total Medical Staff was fifty, of which twenty were Marine Hospital Service surgeons.

Boards of Consulting Experts

A body of twenty-three experienced medical men were chosen amongst the various Wards, who were available at any time for consultation upon difficult or suspicious cases.

During the first few days after the Marine Hospital Service was officially placed in charge of the campaign, Dr. White was busy meeting the Presidents of the Ward organisations, placing his own officers in charge of the Wards, instructing them in their duties, and holding daily conferences with the various representative bodies.

On August 11 he met the Presidents of the Ward Organisations and agreed upon the following general plans :—

That the work of the Ward Organisation must be carried on as strenuously in the future as in the past.

That there should be a "mosquito-killing day" throughout the city once a week, when the entire population should make an effort to kill by fumigation the mosquitos in their houses.

That all street gutters should be flushed out once a week.

That every Ward undertake a complete minute inspection of all cisterns in its territory to see that they are perfectly screened.

That as an extra precaution the oilings of all cisterns be continued.

That only oil of at least 150 flash test be used, so as not to render water unpleasant.

That all physicians and every one else in the city report to headquarters every suspicious case they might learn of.

The experts then issued a series of directions upon :—

1. The formation of oiling, screening, inspecting and salting squads.

2. Upon hourly reporting to headquarters.

3. Upon how to fumigate.

4. Necessity of reporting suspicious cases.

5. Necessity of systematic sanitary surveys.

6. That there is only one Authority in the city.

7. Warning against quack remedies.

All these directions emphasised those which had already been issued by the local authorities.

Result of Campaign.—Yellow fever broke out in an unprepared densely populated city (New Orleans) in July. By August 12 the fever was at its height, numbering on that day 105 cases. In the meantime the prophylactic measures, including early notification, isolation, fumigation, screening, and protection of the water supplies, had begun to take effect, for in three weeks from the notification of the first case the number of fresh cases ceased increasing and it was clear the fever was in hand. The infected stegomyias on the wing had been killed and would no longer carry infection, and a fresh supply of stegomyias was rendered impossible owing to the fact that all cisterns had been screened. Thus an outbreak which in previous years would have developed into the usual awful epidemic was in a few weeks at a comparatively small cost completely stopped, and that in the face of a dense population, open drains, and a sultry summer.

12

ANTI - YELLOW FEVER MEASURES IN BRITISH
HONDURAS AND IN THE ADJACENT CENTRAL
AMERICAN REPUBLICS

In the summer of 1905, whilst I was then taking
part in the yellow fever campaign in New Orleans, I
was asked by the Colonial Office to proceed to Belize
to investigate an outbreak of yellow fever there, and
to report upon measures to stamp it out and prevent
its reappearance.

I gladly availed myself of the opportunity, and
commenced investigations on September 17, 1905.

My first care was to ascertain to what extent the
epidemic had gained a foothold, or, in other words,
the total number and distribution of the human
carriers. I was soon satisfied that the officially reported cases did not represent the total cases—that, in
other words, a considerable number of "suspects"
should have been added to the list. At the same
time I hastened to ascertain the extent and distribution in the town of the insect carriers. I made at
once a stegomyia survey, organising for that purpose
small search parties to ascertain accurately the breeding places of the stegomyia, and so determine the
numerical strength of the insect. To this end we
made a house-to-house investigation and examined
1,342 barrels containing water, many hundreds of kerosene tins, 489 large wooden water-vats, 271 iron water-
tanks, 91 wells, and very many other likely places, such
as disused canoes, ditches, pools, crab-holes, etc. This
examination revealed the presence of the stegomyia

breeding grounds in 50 per cent. of the houses and yards. The water most favoured by the mosquito for her eggs was the clean water for domestic use stored in the cisterns, barrels, tins, and odd receptacles mentioned above, and not the water of the pools, ditches, marshes, or crab-holes. This survey proved at once that the insect carriers were everywhere to hand in and around the houses, and that therefore the ideal conditions for the spread of the disease were present.

As a result I reported upon the absolute necessity of exercising a vigilant supervision over the water supply of the town—that is to say, removing and destroying all odd water receptacles and encouraging the use of proper screened domestic and public cisterns.

I am glad to say that the work commenced by me in 1905 has borne fruit, for by a report of the United States medical officer, dated March 27, 1907, it is stated that in Belize much is being done to render the town as sanitary as possible. The tanks are carefully screened, and unscreened water-barrels and other breeding places of stegomyia have been removed from most of the premises. Two sanitary inspectors are constantly employed to examine into and report upon the proper carrying out of the regulations bearing on these points. Then the streets are kept clean, and work is constantly progressing towards eliminating the breeding-places of mosquitos; mosquitos are not constantly present in great numbers; and since the screening and cleaning ordinance has been systematically carried out, the number of stegomyia has been reduced to a very marked extent. Nor has it been necessary since my visit to quarantine on account of yellow fever any ship leaving the port of Belize, and this has meant a very considerable saving of money, not to mention loss of lives.

In further confirmation of the efficiency of this campaign, the Hon. Wilfred Collet, Colonial Secretary, British Honduras, writes me that in 1907 an epidemic of dengue fever broke out in the Colony. Naturally a disease like dengue caused a very considerable amount of uneasiness, on account of its close resemblance to yellow fever, and as a result the Marine Hospital Service of the United States made a most searching inquiry. Their representatives, however, reported that there were *no stegomyia* to be found, and the disease could not be yellow fever ! The result was that the United States authorities at once permitted the usual trade facilities between the Southern States and Belize. No ship was detained, and the commerce of the port was not interfered with. In 1908, after a very close season, the water-vats warped and the staves opened, as not infrequently happens ; the result was that the stegomyia began to appear again. The authorities, however, immediately instituted a vigorous screening campaign, which was followed by a disappearance of the stegomyia in two months' time.

SPANISH HONDURAS

PUERTO CORTES—ANTIMOSQUITO WORK

We may take this small fruit port as a further example of other similar ones where the work of warfare against mosquitos has begun to be carried on with considerable vigour in Central America. The population of the town numbers about 2,400. The existence of yellow fever would close down the considerable trade which is done in the exportation of fruit to the United States, hence the necessity for war against the stegomyia; and in July 1907 the United States medical officer reported that the authorities had oiled all water-containers—viz. 113 cisterns, 167 barrels, and 26 wells, and that all surface pools were either drained or oiled thoroughly. Result that stegomyia was reported not numerous.

ANTI-YELLOW FEVER CAMPAIGN IN THE CANAL ZONE

This campaign was pushed forward with great vigour from the moment that the Isthmian Canal Commissioners took over the health administration of the Zone.

The plan of campaign lay in rigorously prohibiting the keeping of stagnant water, and in screening, house-to-house inspection, and the infliction of fines if larvæ were discovered. As the result, yellow fever has been banished. Colonel Gorgas, under whose able direction these successful operations have been carried out, writes in his 1908 Report that " it is now more than three years since a case of yellow fever has developed in the Isthmus, the last case occurring in November 1905. The health and sick rates will compare favourably with most parts of the United States." Surely a most successful campaign.

THE ANTI-YELLOW FEVER CAMPAIGN IN RIO JANEIRO AND SANTOS, 1903

In a very delightful tract entitled "Comment on assainit un Pays"[1]—or the extinction of yellow fever in Rio—will be found the results obtained to-day by the vigorous war against the stegomyia which has been waged since 1903.

Brazil has usually been regarded as the home of yellow fever. We have already seen how, in the remarkable wanderings of the famous ship *Hankey*, bound from Siam to the Antilles, there was an account of her putting into some port in Brazil, and how from that fact we concluded that the so-called "maladie de Siam" should be more appropriately called "maladie de Brésil." On the other hand, those of Brazil blame the Antilles for the introduction of the disease in the seventeenth century. But, however that may be, fresh doses of the infection came at successive intervals as trade grew. Great epidemics resulted in consequence. Thus we read of great outbreaks in 1850, 1851, 1852. In 1899 the mortality from the disease was 35,557. This great death rate was just at the time when Brazil was expanding, just when large numbers of young men, labourers and clerks, had been attracted from the Old World to the new country—" conquistadores " of commerce—it was amongst the new-comers that the mortality was so high, just as of yore. It also became evident about the year 1883 that yellow

By Rangel Pestana.

fever could no longer be regarded as a seaport disease, for it went into the interior and up into the hills. The situation had about this time become exceedingly serious; Brazil had gained a bad name for itself— a white man's grave, "Tombeau des étrangers," a place where yellow jack was endemic. Therefore the Government set to work, offered prizes and encouraged investigators, but alas, all in vain. Thus in 1891 there were 4,456 deaths, 4,312 deaths in 1894, 4,852 deaths in 1898, and so on, mounting up until it could be said that at the end of thirteen years the capital had lost 28,078 victims from yellow jack. Since 1850 this disease has cut off 58,335 lives.

The time of the deliverance of Brazil from this scourge was, however, approaching. It came from the moment Reed, Carroll, Agramonte, and Lazear risked their lives to prove the new doctrine. This done, the Havana theory was taken up *con amore*, and with such enthusiasm that four gentlemen of Rio, Domingo Pereira Vaz, Oscar Marques Moreira, Januario Fiori, and André Ramos, together with Dr. Emilio Ribas, submitted also to be bitten by infected mosquitos. The results were, as at Havana, a complete demonstration of the stegomyia doctrine. Furthermore, numerous other experiments were made, and all proved the one thing,—that yellow fever could only be transmitted by one particular mosquito, *the stegomyia*.

The result was a vigorous antistegomyia policy under Dr. Oswaldo Cruz, and the pushing aside of all doubters. Antimosquito brigades were formed.

One brigade consisted of 1,500 men to wage relentless war upon all the breeding places of the stegomyia. All stagnant water was upset, all useless receptacles removed to the dust tip, and houses scaled to clear the gutters. A rapidly moving column was organised to deal instantly with any house in which infected mosquitos might be ; they were attacked at once with sulphur and pyrethrum.

Thus it came about that between the years 1903–1906, a period when everything, according to the old doctrines, should have engendered yellow fever—viz. open putrefying drains, mud dredging, moisture, a close fœtid atmosphere—in fact, a period of the old-time concatenation of circumstances when miasm ought to be distilled and deal death all around, passed in perfect safety ; more emigrants than ever arrived, but no yellow fever. A total of 948 deaths in 1904 showed that ignorance had been at last conquered, and that never again could there be room for doubt. And for once the strong arm of the law felt it had reason on its side ; it did not hesitate to punish those who transgressed and were found harbouring the enemy — the stegomyia larvæ.

As evidence of the earnestness of the people we read that in 1909 153,670 breeding places of larvæ were destroyed, 850,575 odd water receptacles examined, as well as 44,343 reservoirs and 604,283 water-containers overhauled ; as many as 814,650 sinks and 718,154 water-closets oiled ; 2,545 cartloads of tins and odd receptacles were removed from yards. For fumigation 1,242 kilos of pyrethrum and 28,603 kilos of sulphur were used. And this brought it about that in the summer of 1909, in spite of the arrival of some 45,219 new-comers, the word went forth that yellow fever no longer existed in Rio. Can any one in his right mind, after a demonstration like this, afford to doubt and thwart the efforts of those who believe ?

As with Rio, so with Santos : once the white man's death trap, it has now become a veritable " santos " or health resort. Yet in the harbours of Rio and Santos ships once rotted and fell to pieces for want of crews— all had died of the accursed disease ; and to-day no one fears, and no ship rots.

ANTI-YELLOW FEVER CAMPAIGN ON THE AMAZON [1]

Since April 1905, when the Liverpool School of Tropical Medicine dispatched a commission consisting of Drs. Thomas and Breinl, a great deal has been done to disseminate the knowledge of the danger of the stegomyia amongst the merchants trading at Iquitos, Para, Manos, etc. The mission has received the warm support of the trading firms, and it is hoped that under Dr. Thomas a still greater amelioration of the health conditions will be brought about, and yellow fever banished. In 1905 Dr. Thomas published in Spanish a useful Report upon the Public Health of Iquitos. He found the *Stegomyia calopus* present everywhere in water-barrels and odd receptacles throughout

---

[1] The first yellow fever expedition sent out by the school was in 1900, and consisted of Drs. Durham and Walter Myers. The latter investigator contracted and died from the disease

the town. He drew up recommendations urging compulsory screening, removal of odd receptacles, and cleansing of yards.

THE ANTI-YELLOW FEVER OPERATIONS IN THE BRITISH WEST INDIES, 1906–1909

It was to be expected that these ancient Colonies would follow the brilliant examples set them by Cuba and on the Spanish Main by the Isthmian Canal Zone, and endeavour to put their house in order so as to be able to withstand yellow fever and banish malaria. I have referred in a preceding chapter to the awful mortality which yellow fever produced in the 'fifties, a mortality so great that to-day we cannot realise it. In those days the West Indies were regarded as the home of yellow fever, the islands where it was endemic. The adjacent American Continent regarded the islands as the source of all their epidemics. When discussing the march of general sanitation we showed how both the yellow fever and malaria abated before the modern weapons of drainage and water supplies. Abated, however, only to a certain degree, just as in Rio and in many other parts of the world. The really significant change did not occur until the newest weapons of medical science were unerringly directed against the specific enemies—the stegomyia in the case of yellow fever and the anophelines in the case of malaria. Then, and only then, were these diseases brought under absolute control.

I wish in this narrative to state what those islands which I have already visited have accomplished : how

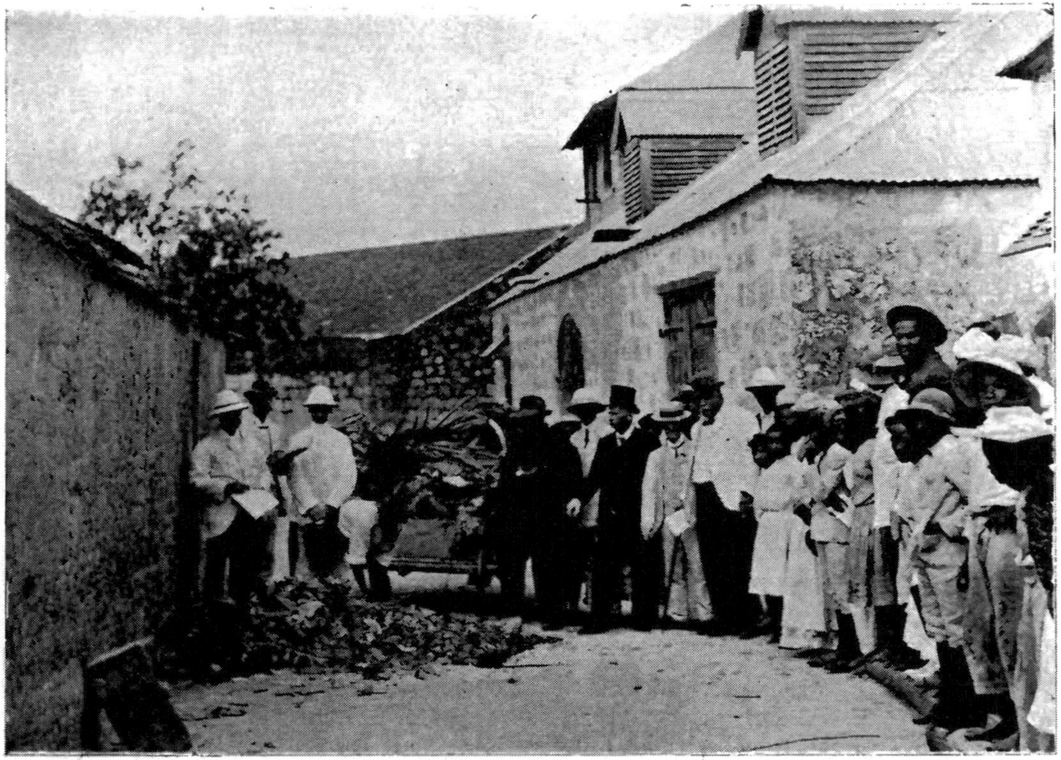

FIG. 35.—THE ANTIMOSQUITO BRIGADE, BRIDGETOWN, BARBADOS, 1900.

far their methods are modern, whether they are still hampered by prejudice and tradition, or are willing to embrace the modern method.

In the first place I will begin by giving my methods of procedure when I arrive in a colony.

1. I establish an office or headquarters, or secretarial department, where the plan of campaign is drawn up with the assistance of the local medical and health authorities.

2. The mornings are devoted to a house-to-house examination of the locality in order to determine precisely the number of breeding places of the stegomyia, in the case of yellow fever. I invariably make the house-to-house inspection with the district medical officers and all the sanitary inspectors available, together with the chairman and others of the Sanitary Boards of the district in which I am working. The more who accompany me on these inspections the better, for they all learn the methods and their significance. When we enter a house with a yard and garden, every water-container is carefully examined and the results entered in the Special Inspection Book. Nothing is neglected : the water receptacles for the chickens— the " Café de Poule "—the water for the dog or other animals, the drinking-water barrels, the washing-tubs, and the innumerable odds and ends, are all carefully examined for the larvæ of the stegomyia. By this means a correct estimate of the percentage of the breeding places is worked out, and the efficacy of the work accomplished by the medical authority in charge gauged.

Whilst making these investigations, ample opportunity is afforded of talking with the householders and of explaining to them the significance of the visit and the necessity for the removal of all stagnant water in and out of doors. An estimate is at the same time made of the general cleanliness of the interior and exterior of the house, and if there are any broken bottles or odd tins about the yard, the householder is admonished to remove them at once. For this special purpose we are frequently accompanied by the dust contractor and his carts.

To sum up the results of my house-to-house inspections in the West Indies, I examined—

525 yards in Bridgetown, Barbados,
 48   ,,   ,, Georgetown, Demerara,
211   ,,   ,, in Port of Spain, Trinidad,
 72   ,,   ,, in Castries, St. Lucia,
 98   ,,   ,, in Kingston, Grenada,
125   ,,   ,, in St. Vincent.

In these yards I found and examined a total of 2,292 water receptacles; these included 574 buckets, 425 barrels, 695 tubs, 392 jars, 114 large tins and cans, 92 vats, also an innumerable number of odd receptacles such as broken bottles and pitchers, small tins, conch shells, calabashes, flower vases, saucers, lily tubs, etc. etc. When mosquito larvæ were found, they were those of the *Stegomyia calopus*.

Nature of the Water-containers.—Each Colony had for the most part its own peculiarities in the way of water-containers. Wherever barrels were used for

Fig. 36.—THE RUBBISH-CART BRIGADE, BRIDGETOWN, BARBADOS, 1909.

the storage of water, as in straggling districts and small villages, larvæ were always most abundant. In Castries and in other Colonies which were formerly under French rule, the large old-fashioned jars were the great offenders. In George Town, Demerara, vats predominate. In Port of Spain, Trinidad, the antiformicas, as I have previously explained, are a source of danger.

It was abundantly evident from my visits that in all these six Colonies measures had been taken to abate the stegomyia breeding nuisance. First and foremost, a pipe-borne water supply is now the rule, but it wants further extension. Secondly, the town councils have been fairly active in removing all odds and ends from yards likely to contain water. Thirdly, in all these Colonies health clauses have been inserted dealing specifically with the stagnant-water nuisance— the presence of larvæ being taken as proof of this. Fines are inflicted regularly for infringement of these bylaws. Screening is compulsory in some places. Fourthly, in many places an active antimosquito propaganda has been set on foot and the people have been educated. Fifthly, both the medical officers and the sanitary inspectors have in many places been trained either in tropical diseases at the Tropical Schools in England, or, as in the case of the sanitary inspectors, they have been trained to recognise and differentiate the various mosquito larvæ and to realise their significance. In addition to these antilarval measures, the health authorities have also clauses to deal with the fumigation of houses in which yellow fever has occurred, the screening of patients, and early notification. Had these West Indian Colonies not already commenced to make these reforms that brought them into line with Cuba and the Canal Zone, there can be little doubt that they would have been visited by epidemics of yellow fever which in former days were, as we have seen, the rule. The best test of this is the recent epidemic in Barbados. This epidemic has been kept under; it was practically stamped out in May in the chief port, Bridgetown, whereas in former days it would have gone on gaining in force and virulence. The fever persisted longer in the straggling isolated country parishes around because the machinery for carrying out thorough fumigation was not so complete as in the chief town. One of the West India Islands has been very severely visited by yellow fever, viz. the French Colony of Martinique, and in this island we have evidence that antilarval measures had not been vigorously pushed. Yet, in spite of the fact that yellow fever was raging in Martinique, the adjacent island of St. Lucia remained absolutely secure owing entirely to the wise antilarval measures and sharp look-out taken by the Governor and his officers. It proves conclusively that yellow fever need never again be a source of alarm to the West Indies as of old, provided that anti-larval measures are pushed. Again, a source of great danger to the West Indian group is Venezuela, the remaining stronghold of yellow fever. But, again, the adjacent Colony of Trinidad, with its up-to-date antimosquito measures, need have little to fear. In this respect the " Liver-

FIG. 37.—COLLECTION OF ODD WATER RECEPTACLES, THE WORK OF A FEW DAYS. BRIDGETOWN, BARBADOS.

p. 190]

pool" of the West Indies (Port of Spain) has as little to dread as the Liverpool of Lancashire. Nevertheless, no Colony can afford to take risks, and as rigid an inspection of all arrivals from Venezuela must be made as the Isthmian Canal authorities enforce in the case of arrivals into their territory. In other words, each Colony must see that all its defences are perfect. In the present day, with our knowledge of how yellow fever is carried, its presence in any Colony is rightly regarded as a disgrace, and as showing that the Colony is as yet in the barbarous stage, and possesses no medical organisation worthy of the name. Yellow fever is not to-day regarded as the inevitable penalty of our desire to go to tropical lands; it is to-day the penalty of ignorance and superstition.

Finally, as the result of my investigation of the numerical strength of the breeding places of the stegomyia, I found the rate was not high, varying from 4 to 10 per cent.[1] But this percentage must be reduced to zero. In the Appendix will be found collected together those health clauses of the various Colonies which I visited which deal with anti-yellow fever and antimalarial warfare; they are useful as a guide to other Colonies which may not have yet come into line. These measures, and the numerous penalties which followed their systematic enforcement, constitute the most eloquent testimony which we possess of the

---

[1] In a letter which I have received as I go to press from Dr. Hudson of Barbados, there is the gratifying statement that "The first fortnightly returns of mosquito destruction in the parishes shows that only 0·45 per cent. of the houses inspected were found to be harbouring larvæ." This is a remarkably good result.

earnestness of this great health campaign in the West Indian Colonies.

Thus in Trinidad there have been 29 prosecutions from March to April of 1909 ; 98 in St. Lucia from 1907-9 ; 99 in Barbados during April and May of 1909 ; and the fines have ranged from 1*s.* to 40*s.*

DENGUE OR DANDY FEVER

This is a tropical fever of wide distribution, occurring in the West Indies, Syria, the Far East, India, Australasia, Central and South America. In the present day it owes a considerable amount of its importance to the fact that, together with influenza, it is liable to be confused with yellow fever. Like the latter fever, it appears to follow the trade routes and to burst out without warning into considerable-sized epidemics of an essentially local character. Indeed, in its mode of extension and its tendency to keep to the coast line, it resembles an insect-borne disease, and evidence is accumulating in favour of this view. Thus Dr. H. Graham of Beyrouth has brought forward reasons which show that dengue fever is spread by the *Culex fatigans*. This observer states that he was able to infect (1901) healthy persons by the bite of infected mosquitos, that is, mosquitos which had bitten patients suffering from the disease.

Dr. Strong of Manilla likewise (1909) states that recent studies in Manilla point to the *Culex fatigans* as the transmitting agent, and I have received a note from the Hon. W. Collett, Colonial Secretary, British

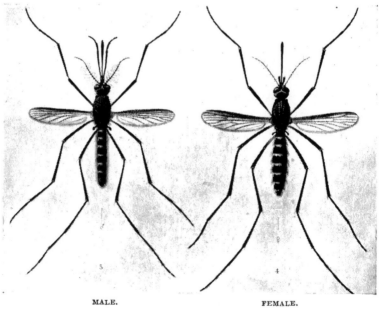

MALE.   FEMALE.

FIG. 38.—CULEX FATIGANS.

Honduras, concerning an outbreak of dengue fever in that Colony, in which he states :

" An epidemic of dengue broke out in the middle of the year 1907, and P.M.O. Harrison estimated that 45 per cent. of the population suffered. A few who had previously had yellow fever contracted the disease, so that evidently yellow fever does not protect. It was noted that wherever dengue fever occurred the *Culex fatigans* was also found. Mr. Collett had the culex in his own house, and his youngest child contracted the disease ; both himself and Mrs. Collett, however, escaped, as they had had the disease in Fiji in 1885."

PART II

CHAPTER XV

TRYPANOSOMIASIS (SLEEPING SICKNESS)

THIS morbid condition, better known in one of its forms in man as sleeping sickness, belongs to that group of diseases, including malaria, filariasis, and tick fever, which are caused by minute animal parasites living in the blood stream of the body. Like, also, many of the other tropical diseases, it attacks a wide range of the animal kingdom. I have had occasion to refer to this significant fact before. We will have noted that these diseases are not peculiar to man alone; man is simply liable to them just as are other species of the animal kingdom.

Naturally, when man is affected in epidemic form, our attention is at once directed to the disease, and investigations made and the cause discovered. It was thus with sleeping sickness. The trypanosome, as the small blood parasite which causes the disease is called, was discovered in 1902, but long before that date

194

(1869) it had already been known as a blood parasite in many of the lower animals. In 1901 Dr. Dutton, of the Liverpool School, whilst investigating tropical diseases in the Gambia Colony, discovered the parasite in the blood of a patient, exhibiting no unusual symptoms, under the care of Dr. Forde, and he named it the *Trypanosoma gambiense*; and then, in the year 1902, the world was made aware by Bruce and Castellani of the fact that the mysterious and deadly disease which was rapidly spreading over Central Africa—Sleeping Sickness—was due to the same parasite.   Since then the disease has been subjected to numerous investigations (see Appendix), and international action has been taken to endeavour to limit its ravages and if possible stamp it out.   It would appear that the disease has only attained its present prominence in Africa comparatively recently, coincident with the opening up of Africa to development, consequently necessitating the formation of trade routes and the movement of large bodies of natives from point to point.   The disease, if it existed amongst the natives in earlier times, remained confined to circumscribed areas ; in opening up trade, however, the disease diffused itself, and is still doing so, until it is said to extend over some million square miles.   The spread of this disease has wiped out entire communities, large districts have been depopulated in the Congo, 200,000 of the inhabitants of the Uganda Protectorate are believed to have perished.

The question naturally arises, How does the disease spread ?   Is it by contact, by water and food, or by insects ?   Knowing as much as we now do about the spread of tropical diseases, we are not surprised to learn that this disease is spread by the agency of an insect. This time a fly—the well-known tsetse fly. Bruce had previously proved that the fly disease of horses and cattle known as Nagana in Africa was communicated from animal to animal by the bite of a species of fly (*Glossina morsitans*); he concluded, moreover, that the transference was mechanical—that is to say that, unlike the case of the malarial parasite where the anophelines play the part of intermediary hosts, the fly simply became mechanically infected by the parasite adhering to the mouth parts, so that when it bit a healthy animal it transferred to the wound the adherent parasites, in a manner somewhat analogous to the way in which the domestic house-fly carries infection on its body. The mode of infection having been shown in Nagana, it was not long before it was determined that an allied species of fly (*Glossina palpalis*) was probably the agent which transmitted sleeping sickness.

There was here, as in the case of yellow fever and malaria, the most significant fact that sleeping sickness was found only in districts where the fly was found. No tsetse, no sleeping sickness : just as no anophelines, no malaria ; no stegomyia, no yellow fever.

In the West Indies, where although there are many species of biting flies there is no tsetse, sleeping sickness has not occurred.

The next great question then arose, Was the transference of infection mechanical ? Or, as in malaria and yellow fever, did the fly act as host ?

[*Photo by Dr. W. H. Graham.*

FIG. 39.—GLOSSINA PALPALIS, THE CARRIER OF SLEEPING
SICKNESS. Enlarged Four Times.

Block lent by S S Bureau.

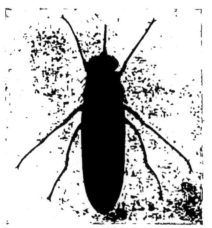

FIG. 41.—NATURAL SIZE OF
TSETSE FLY.

[*Photo by Dr. W. M. Graham.*

FIG. 40.—GLOSSINA FUSCA, IN RESTING POSITION.
Enlarged about Three Times.

Block lent by S. S. Bureau.

p. 196]

Did, in other words, the parasite pass part of its life cycle in the fly, as did the malaria parasite in the mosquito? The answer, as - furnished by the experiments of Kleine and Bruce, point to the conclusion that, much as in the case of yellow fever virus in the stegomyia, a latent period exists in the fly during which period it is not infectious, but that after the period of latency, the fly becomes again infectious. In the case of the Sleeping Sickness parasites the latent period appears to be from 14 to 21 days. These observations point to the fact that the fly acts as a true host to the trypanosome just as the anophelines do to the parasite of malaria ; in other words, the fly appears necessary to the propagation of the disease.

Plan of Campaign.—Having proved that the tsetse fly is the carrier of sleeping sickness, and proved moreover, as it would appear from the most recent observations, that it is only one species, the *Glossina palpalis*, that can act as host to the trypanosome, we have the key of the plan of preventing the disease altogether, viz. by exterminating the carrier, precisely as in the plan of campaign against malaria, yellow fever, and plague.

The tsetse fly, like the common house fly and like the mosquito, has its two phases—the adult winged form and the larval form. It can be attacked at both stages, whichever is most practical or most convenient.

In the first place, observations have shown that the breeding place of the fly is the strip of ground bush along the rivers ; a strip about 30 yards wide extending from the river-bank is the usual breeding zone; breeding appears not to extend to any marked degree beyond this distance.

The larval or pupa stage evidently requires a certain amount of humidity and shade, and requires to be protected from the direct sun-rays, and hence the fly chooses the damp shaded humus of the bush in which to deposit her pupæ. Therefore, as a first step in prophylaxis, it is necessary to destroy the ground bush, to burn it for a depth of about 30 yards from the river-bank.

It is not necessary to cut down forests any more than it is necessary to drain lakes and run rivers dry in antimalarial operations. All that is essential is to go for the chief breeding grounds around man and to let the forests take care of themselves.

The reason is precisely similar to that which we fully discussed under malaria and yellow fever. We cannot attempt the impossible, and it is totally unnecessary; the object is to protect man in his villages and towns and camps and along his trade routes, and this can be done. It is, as we have so often emphasised, a question of protecting man against his innumerable insect surroundings. In practice this has been found to be perfectly feasible, as easy as preventing the keeping of stagnant water in and around houses in yellow fever countries or getting rid of pools and anopheline breeding grounds around the houses in malaria countries, or destroying cover for rats in seaport towns.

What is therefore now done is to burn the ground

bush along the margins of rivers and ponds and around encampments and villages, and to keep the roads clear. The sun's heat has a most detrimental effect on the fly and prevents them breeding in such situations. Further, as in the case of the mosquito, the natural enemies of the fly are to be encouraged. These consist of both the enemies of the adult fly and those of the pupæ, and amongst them are described certain birds, wasps, spiders, ants, and fungi. The collection and destruction of the pupæ have also been advocated. The drainage of pools in the vicinity of camps and villages is also of use.

The destruction of wild animals which the fly may use for sucking blood, such as the crocodile, is also advocated.

Having disposed of the method of attack as regards the breeding grounds of the fly, let us examine what can be done against the adult insect. In this connection a series of regulations have been adopted as follows :—

Protect the body as much as possible from un- necessary exposure to the bite of the fly—

(a) by wearing plenty of suitable clothing (white),

(b) by systematic use of nets,

(c) by screening the living-rooms,

(d) by choosing for the sites of houses and encamp- ments places free from flies,

(e) avoiding fly-infected routes.

In all these rational and practical measures, the lines followed are those which we have seen accomplish so much in malaria and yellow fever. And as in the case of yellow fever, so here a great deal can be done by rational quarantine administration. Natives coming from infected districts should not be allowed to freely travel into non-infected districts. They must be subjected to most careful medical inspection to ascertain whether they have the parasite in their blood or not, and those who have must be detained and isolated in properly screened hospitals. The principle of segregation should also be adopted where possible. The healthy should live at a distance from the villages or the huts of those who may be suspected to have the parasites.

Lastly, as in malaria, an endeavour can be made to kill the parasites in the blood. In malaria use is made of quinine, in sleeping sickness the great drug is arsenic in some form or other; therefore *arsenisation* is a great curative and prophylactic measure of defence, and is having good results. According to authorities like Koch and Manson, arsenic in the form of atoxyl is as efficacious in early cases of sleeping sickness as quinine is in malaria.

Upon these lines of attack a great anti-sleeping sickness campaign has been undertaken by all the nations possessing Central African colonies.

In order to direct the operations of the campaign in British Africa, a National Bureau has been established in London, and at these headquarters regular monthly reports are issued and reports collected from all sleeping sickness districts, maps are made and issued showing the progress of the disease and the districts' of the fly. The Bureau, which has been established under the auspices of the Colonial Office, has already done excellent service, and the system might well be copied in the case of the other tropical diseases.

Although it is early yet to speak of the results of the anti-sleeping sickness measures, there is no question that much good work has been already done and very many lives saved ; they serve as indications of what can be done. The following Report received from the Governor of Uganda shows clearly that improvement is taking place :

RESULT OF ANTI-SLEEPING SICKNESS MEASURES IN UGANDA
(From *Manchester Guardian*, June 25, 1909)

The Governor of Uganda in his Report for 1907-8 to the Earl of Crewe (Secretary for the Colonies) is able to report that the measures taken during the past three years to stamp out sleeping sickness are proving effectual.   During 1907 the deaths in the Kingdom of Buganda numbered less than 4,000, and in 1908 they fell to 1,700.   It is believed (the Governor says) that for the whole Protectorate the deaths during the past twelve years have not exceeded 2,500. No Europeans have been infected since 1906.   Practically the whole of the population of the fly-infested shores of Lake Victoria have been removed to districts inland, where the tsetse does not exist, and it is believed that there can now be but few cases of fresh infection so far as the mainland is concerned.   Steps are in progress for the complete depopulation of the islands in the Lake.   It was feared that this would prove a most difficult matter, but the native Government is now showing such confidence in the efficacy of the measures for the suppression of the sickness that the request for final action has come from them. About 21,000 souls will have to be moved, and arrangements are being made to locate them on vacant lands in Chagwe and in other districts of the mainland. The realisation of this project will put the finishing touch to the whole scheme.

The pestilent tsetse fly will still infest the shores of the great Lake, but it will find no more victims on which to play its malevolent part. Sleeping sickness has ceased to be the dominant scourge of this territory, and the disease has now been reduced to a merely sporadic scale. Continued vigilance, however, is essential, and the recrudescence of sleeping sickness can only be averted by the consistent and vigorous maintenance of those preventive measures which have already proved efficacious. The four segregation camps, in which several thousands of sufferers are still located, are in full working order, and though no effective curative treatment has yet been discovered, the lives of many of the patients are being considerably prolonged. The measures taken to drive away the tsetse flies from the neighbourhood of Entebbe and of other important points on the Lake shore, from which the population could not be removed, have proved successful, and those places may now be considered perfectly safe, so far as sleeping sickness is concerned.

The Principal Medical Officer, A. D. P. Hodges, furnishes the following satisfactory statement from Uganda :—

" I think that the continued and progressive decrease in the death rate, which is apparent in the returns from individual counties as well as in the totals, is scarcely likely to have been artificially contrived or to be a mere coincidence. I, therefore, regard it as a true decrease and as decidedly satisfactory and encouraging; for, even though the actual figures may be inexact, the rate of decrease shown is in all probability substantially a true one.

" It will be noticed that the decrease on the mainland has been much greater in 1907 and 1908 than in 1905 and 1906, while the difference between these two periods is much less marked in the case of the islands.

" This decrease must be attributed to the preventive measures which were begun in 1906 on the mainland, and they have produced a fall in the deathrate from 3,585 in 1906, to 1,419 in 1907."

" Making full allowance for other causes, unless we are to place no reliance at all on the Chiefs' returns, the conclusion can scarcely be avoided, in my opinion, that the preventive measures which have been applied are producing results so satisfactory as to warrant their continuance wherever practicable and their extension wherever this is possible."

DEATHS FROM SLEEPING SICKNESS IN BUGANDA KINGDOM

Year	Mainland	Islands.	Totals	Mainland.	Islands	Totals
1905	4,500	3,503	8,003	8,085	5,222	13,307
1906	3,515	1,719	5,304			
1907	1,419	1,992	3,407	1,965	3,165	5,130
1908	550	1,173	1,723			
	10,054	8,387	18,437	—	—	18,437

THE SEPTIC FLY (*MUSCA DOMESTICA*)

The awakening of interest in insects as carriers of disease by the study of the tropical diseases malaria, yellow fever, and plague and tsetse fly disease, has been chiefly instrumental in drawing our attention to the danger of the common house fly. Recently Howard of Washington has proposed to substitute the name "typhoid fly" instead of house fly. He is indeed justified in doing so, for there is overwhelming proof that the house fly is one of the important carriers of that disease. It has been more especially during military campaigns that evidence to this effect on a vast scale has been forthcoming, but in the case of villages and towns we have abundant evidence also of the activity of the fly in spreading typhoid. Inasmuch, however, as the common fly is equally able to transmit cholera, tuberculosis, and the various intestinal bacteria associated with the diarrhœa prevalent in towns in summer time, I think the term "Septic Fly" would be more appropriate.

It has for long been believed that the fly can carry disease germs, that it is a mechanical carrier. Every one must have observed that the fly is a filth-eater. What dust-bin, what garbage, exists without the fly? We become aware that something is wrong or rotten, by the presence of flies. We must have all experienced the dread with which we have seen the common fly in the sick-room. Wherever there is rotting, fermentation, or decay, or, in other words, animal or vegetable. offal or excreta of any kind,

Fig. 42.—MASS OF FLY LARVÆ IN STABLE MANURE. (Natural Size.)

[*R. Newstead.*

p. 204]

there the fly must be. Why? Because as the water-barrel is to the larva of the stegomyia and the earth-pool to the larvæ of the anophelines, so is putrid, fermenting material to the larvæ or maggots of the fly. The fly breeds there, deposits its eggs there, and they hatch out into the well-known maggots. It is not surprising, then, that the natural breeding grounds being filthy material, the fly should carry on its body some of this filth to the sugar basin, the entrée dish, or the milk in the bowl in the pantry. Unquestionably the fly can and does contaminate our food supplies, and by landing on the face around the eyes and mouth it may directly inoculate disease germs. Beauperthuy long ago directed attention to this. The presence of flies in a house means that filth is close at hand—not miles away, but, in all probability, close outside the kitchen window in the dust-bin, or in the adjacent stables, or in the highly manured garden soil around the house.

We must have often observed by the sea foreshore the prevalence of flies especially where the foreshore is used as a dumping ground for garbage. Yet town councils have wondered why their apparently beauti-fully situated seaside resorts should still have cases of typhoid and other intestinal fevers. There is no wonder when we realise that the fly is the common carrier. The fly has now been proved experimentally to be a carrier in the case of cholera, typhoid, tubercle, and no doubt of the germs of summer diarrhœa. In Egypt the dissemination of the common ophthalmia present amongst the poor people is also largely due to the fly; for we have no doubt seen in that country the eyes of children rendered black by swarms of them. The relationship of the fly to leprosy has often been commented upon, and in my own experience I have on many occasions been struck by the great abundance of flies swarming around the patients.

Plan of Campaign.—Knowing the danger of the fly, the next step is to get rid of it. As far as I am aware, the first Corporation to move in this direction was that of the City of Liverpool. In December 1906 the Medical Officer of Health of this city, Dr. Hope, instructed Mr. Newstead of the Liverpool School of Tropical Medicine to undertake a minute inquiry into the breeding places of the fly throughout the city. A report was drawn up by Mr. Newstead which has served as a model for many other corporations in this and other countries. The chief strongholds of the fly were found to be manure-heaps in connection with stables and shippons, and ashpits of all kinds. Mr. Newstead found that 25 per cent of ashpits were infected with larvæ. Other breeding places were all odd collections of fermenting material, vegetable or animal, accumulations of manure at the wharves, bedding for poultry, pigs, etc. Mr. Newstead lays stress upon the selective affinity which flies have for human dejecta for feeding purposes, and in this propensity lies of course the great danger of the house fly. It cannot be too clearly understood.

As the results of this investigation Mr. Newstead recommends the following plan of warfare :

1. That stable manure and spent hops should not be allowed to accumulate in the middensteads during the months of May to October inclusive, for *a period of more than seven days*.

2. All middensteads should be thoroughly emptied and carefully swept at the period stated in 1.

The present system of *partly emptying* such receptacles should in all cases be discontinued.

The walls of middensteads should also be cemented over, or, failing this, the brickwork should be sound and well pointed.

3. That all ashpits should be emptied, during the summer months, at intervals of not more than ten days.

4. That the most strenuous efforts should be made to prevent children defæcating in the courts and passages ; or that the parents should be compelled to remove such matter immediately ; and defæcation in stable middens should be strictly forbidden. The danger lies in the overwhelming attraction which such fæcal matter has for house flies, which latter may afterwards come into direct contact with man or his foodstuffs. They may, as Veeder puts it, "in a very few minutes . . . load themselves with dejections from a typhoid or dysenteric patient, not as yet sick enough to be in hospital or under observation, and carry the poison so taken up into the very midst of the food and water ready for use at the next meal. There is no long roundabout process involved."

5. Ashpit refuse, which in any way tends to fermentation, such as bedding, straw, old rags, paper, waste vegetables, dirty bedding from the " hutches " of pet animals, etc., should, if possible, be disposed of by the tenants, preferably by incineration, or be placed

in a separate receptacle so that no fermentation can take place. If such precautions were adopted by householders, relatively few house flies would breed in the ashpits, and the present system of emptying such places at longer intervals than, say, four to six weeks, might be continued.

6. The application of Paris green (poison) at the rate of two ounces to one gallon of water to either stable manure or ashpit refuse will destroy 99 per cent. of the larvæ. Possibly a smaller percentage of Paris green might be employed with equally good results.

One per cent. of crude atoxyl in water kills 100 per cent. of fly larvæ.

The application of either of these substances might, however, lead to serious complications, and it is very doubtful whether they could be employed with safety. Paris green, at the rate of one to two ounces to twenty gallons of water, is used largely as an insecticide for fruit pests. It does no harm to vegetation when applied in small quantities; but cattle might be tempted to eat the dirty straw in manure which had been treated with this substance, and the results might prove fatal if large quantities were eaten.

7. The use of sun-blinds in all shops containing food which attracts flies would, in my opinion, largely reduce the number of flies in such places during hot weather. Small fruiterers' and confectioners' shops, as a rule, are not shaded by sun-blinds, and in their absence flies literally swarm on the articles exposed for sale.

The rules laid down by the Merchants' Associations Committee on pollution of the waters of New York are as follows :

RULES FOR DEALING WITH THE FLY NUISANCE

Keep the flies away from the sick, especially those ill with contagious diseases. Kill every fly that strays into the sick-room. His body is covered with disease germs.

Do not allow decaying material of any sort to accumulate on or near your premises.

All refuse which tends in any way to fermentation, such as bedding, straw, paper waste, and vegetable matter, should be disposed of or covered with lime or kerosene oil.

Screen all food.

Keep all receptacles for garbage carefully covered, and the cans cleaned or sprinkled with oil or lime.

Keep all stable manure in vault or pit, screened or sprinkled with lime, oil, or other cheap preparation.

Cover food after a meal; burn or bury all table refuse.

Screen all food exposed for sale.

Screen all windows and doors, especially the kitchen and dining-room.

Don't forget, if you see flies, their breeding place is in near-by filth. It may be behind the door, under the table or in the cuspidor.

If there is no dirt and filth there will be no flies.

If there is a nuisance in the neighbourhood write at once to the Health Department.

CHAPTER XVI

ANKYLOSTOMIASIS : DIRT CONTAMINATION

ANKYLOSTOMIASIS

THIS is a disease which, like so many of the others which we have described in the preceding pages, teaches a very instructive lesson. It is the disease *par excellence* of workmen and labourers, which breaks out frequently amongst them when they are working and living under insanitary conditions, or rather, not under strict sanitary discipline. Masses of men when left to themselves, away from the intelligent eye of the sanitary officer, revert to the primitive conditions of less civilised nations, or to the condition of our ancestors. In other words, they surely tend to contaminate their surroundings, to " foul their nest," to pollute their houses, villages, water supplies, etc. We know from history how frequently this occurred in the movements of armies in the Middle Ages. It was the frightful mortality from these causes which brought into exist-ence the study of hygiene.

So with ankylostomiasis. This disease has been known for a very considerable time under different names. In Egypt there was a well-marked condition of profound anæmia, which occurred amongst the labouring population, and was known as Egyptian chlorosis. During the construction of the St. Gothard tunnel there broke out an intense anæmia amongst the workmen, which received the name of Tunnel Anæmia. In more recent times severe loss was caused by its extensive prevalence under the name of Miners' Anæmia in the coal mines of Westphalia; and still more recently Professor Haldane has given prominence to it by making accurate observations upon its presence and cause in Cornish mines. In the tropics, under the name Tropical Anæmia, it produces a very great sickness and death rate amongst the labouring classes; this is notably so in India and Ceylon, and to a certain extent amongst the coolie labourers employed in the West Indies. The disease is therefore widely distributed over the globe. Its leading feature is profound anæmia, and the consequences of anæmia—*i.e.* loss of working capacity and invaliding; it is therefore the labour-paralysing disease, and it has in consequence received great attention from scientific observers all over the world, and we are now reaping to the full the benefits of their discoveries. Observers found that, whether the disease was called "tropical," "miner" or "tunnel" anæmia, "Egyptian chlorosis" or "earth-eater's disease," "grounditch" or "hook-worm disease," the cause was one and the same, a small intestinal parasite, the *Ankylostomum duodenale*, which inhabited the intestines in very large numbers and led to a considerable loss of blood in consequence. The eggs of the adult worms were passed in the excreta, and the latter, either not being carefully removed or disinfected, contaminated the water and food supplies of the workmen, or else the abode and ground around the dwellings and villages; it was shown especially by Loos of Cairo that not only could infection take place by means of infected water and food, but that the young worms which had hatched out from the eggs passed in the excreta, in the cane or other plantations surrounding the houses, were capable of penetrating the skin of the barefooted workmen and children and induce the disease. The method of prevention, the plan of campaign, was also made clear from these observations. Obviously the first thing is to prevent the disease spreading by insisting upon the proper treatment of the excreta of the workmen by erecting suitable latrine accommodation, rigorously preventing the pollution of the ground and plantations, etc., around the villages and houses and camps; careful treatment of those suffering from the disease in hospitals and at dispensaries where some intestinal vermifuge and disinfectant of approved efficacy can be obtained. By the use of these drugs the worms are expelled from the intestines and the sufferer rendered non-infectious—just as, in the case of malaria, quinine is employed to kill the parasites in the circulation. By the combination of these wise measures splendid results have been obtained in different parts of the world, and tropical anæmia, like yellow fever and leprosy, will be steadily driven back. In the West Indies the disease is receiving very careful attention; the labourers and their families are, in the first place, very carefully housed and medically cared for; they have good hospitals, where they are promptly treated, and regulations have been framed for their protection. The following extract from a circular issued by C. J. Cox, Colonial Secretary, British Guiana, shows that good work is being done :

" I am directed by the Governor to inform you that in connection with the efforts which have been made by the Government to stamp out Ankylostome infection among East Indian immigrants, it has been found that upon those sugar estates where suitable latrine accommodation has been provided, and where efforts have been made to prevent the resident population from defæcating elsewhere, there has been a marked improvement in health conditions."

But it is to the Philippines under American rule that we must turn for examples of the most extensive safeguarding measures.

THE CAMPAIGN AGAINST ANKYLOSTOMIASIS OR UNCINARIASIS IN PORTO RICO

The permanent commission appointed by the United States to study and institute measures for the prevention and cure of anæmia in Porto Rico has recently issued a report.

" The campaign commenced in 1906–7 ; 35 stations for treatment were established in the island, and a total number of 89,233 patients were treated. The population of the island is 800,000, scattered over an area of 3,306 square miles. It was calculated that

90 per cent. of the population harboured the parasite. To carry out the prophylactic and curative campaign the island was divided into three zones, each under the control of a commissioner. Numerous 'Anæmia Stations' were formed in each district. The diagnosis of each case was made accurately by the use of the microscope. An active educational propaganda was instituted, and the people taught the nature of the disease and how it was contracted; stress was laid upon the necessity of using only privies, and that on no account must the people defæcate on the ground; the people were also exhorted to wear shoes. The treatment consisted in the use of thymol and beta naphthol. The total number of people treated amounted to 89,233; of this number 43 per cent. were cured, and in 16 per cent. the conditions were improved."

It is especially to be noted that the campaign against the ankylostome has a most marked effect in reducing the general death rate. Dr. Heiser, Chief Quarantine Officer for the Philippine Islands, lays great stress upon this aspect of the campaign, and I fully agree. Given a man or woman or child suffering, say, from tuberculosis or other disease, the chances of recovery are immensely decreased if the anæmic condition produced by ankylostomes is also present. If a low mortality rate is desired, then war must be pressed against these parasites.

CHAPTER XVII

MALTA FEVER

Malta Fever.—A bacterial parasitic disease communicated to man chiefly by the milk of goats suffering from this bacterial disease. The germ is a minute micrococcus.

This disease is an excellent example of the principle underlying every previous chapter, and that is the danger of the domestic animal as a source of disease. We have shown that it is the domestic or man-loving mosquito which is to be feared, and which is the very fertile source of spreading diseases. As it is with insects, so with the mammals. From the cow man may be infected with tuberculosis, anthrax, and perhaps scarlet fever, from the horse man may acquire glanders, from the pig trichinosis, and so on. Invariably the higher animals associated with man are liable to suffer from diseases which are also harmful to man, and therefore which they communicate to man by the milk, flesh, or excreta. Malta fever is an exquisite example of this principle. It cannot be too strenuously insisted upon that the domestic economic animals like cattle, swine, and sheep and poultry require hygienic supervision equally with man. Forgetfulness of this principle has over and over again led to the spreading of disease in man. The question can be grappled with in many ways. It can be dealt with as Sir David Bruce dealt with the goats which he found to be the source of the fever in Malta, by either banishing them or their products from man altogether ; or, as in the case of diseased swine, by a most rigorous inspection of the swine flesh as is done in Germany ; or, as in the case of the cow, by a most searching examination for the presence of tubercle in the animal. When it can be carried out, the most effective way is the method employed in the case of Malta fever. It resembles more closely the method used against the mosquito.

But whilst the economic domestic animals are a source of danger to man, it must never be forgotten that the domestic pets of man are also a fertile source of disease. For instance, man may be infected with glanders from the horse, but it is more especially against the dog and cat that man must be on his guard. For example, in Iceland the dog is a very necessary help to the Esquimaux for draught purposes, therefore the dogs are numerous and live close to him, in or around the house. A frequent disorder of these dogs is tape-worm disease ; but, living in such close contact with their employer, man, it is not to be wondered at that man should share the disease with the dogs. It thus comes about that the adult tape-worm phase of this disease is passed in the dog, and the cystic or hydatid phase in man. Similarly with rabies : where dogs are abundant and neglected, there also rabies in man may be expected. The lesson to be learnt from the foregoing facts is that the fewer the domestic pets in and around the dwellings of man the better ; because it stands to reason that, difficult as it is to maintain the health and cleanliness of man, it must necessarily be far more so in the case of cats and dogs, whose wanderings in dirty places can no more be prevented than those of the common fly.

Geographical Distribution.—Malta fever has a wide distribution, producing much suffering and loss of time. It occurs in the islands of the Mediterranean, Italy, Greece, Turkey, Palestine, North Coast of Africa, Cape Colony, Orange River Colony, Arabia, India, China, Philippine Islands, Fiji Islands, North America, West Indies, and South America, etc.

Discovery of Virus and Carrier.—This disease remained a mystery until its nature and significance were worked out by Sir David Bruce, F.R.S., in Malta. In the following account of the results achieved I follow closely the account given by the discoverer of the disease and the author of the simple but absolutely effective prophylactic measures. The virus consists of a small coccus, and is therefore not of the nature of an animal parasite, but belongs to the bacterial group.

Distribution of the Disease in Malta.—The population of the island is about 200,000. The garrison averages about 8,000 troops ; in addition there is a considerable sailor population. Bruce states that almost every native of Malta suffers at one time or another from the disease.

He remarks, " Amongst our troops in the past up

to 1905 the average yearly incidence was 37·6 per thousand. In the year 1905 as many as 403 officers and men were invalided home, and in previous years the numbers were also uniformly high. The average stay of the soldiers and sailors in hospital in Malta was 90 days, and say a further 120 days' stay in hospital when invalided home ; therefore on an average 624 soldiers and sailors were in hospital 120 days each, making up a total of 74,880 days of illness." Bruce adds, " What the amount of personal suffering and loss to the State this sickness and invaliding entailed it is impossible to estimate, but the mere pecuniary loss must have been very considerable."

Discovery of the Virus.—This was found by Bruce to be a microccus—the *Micrococcus melitensis.* Its presence is demonstrable in all persons suffering from the fever.

Discovery of the Source of Infection.—Suspicion fastened upon the goats, which were very plentiful and were the source of the milk supply. Examination of these animals revealed the fact that 50 per cent. of them contained the parasite, although appearing to be perfectly healthy, and in 10 per cent. of them the milk contained the micrococcus. Here then was a magnificent example of so-called " healthy carriers " of the disease, in this case in the animal.

As happened in the case of other infectious processes in man, so here an accidental infection in man gave the final proof. In 1905 a steamer sailing to the States shipped 65 goats from Malta; their milk was consumed by the captain and many of the crew, with the result that an epidemic of Malta fever broke out on the ship, and every one who drank this milk contracted the disease.

Plan of Campaign.—Preventive measures commenced in June 1906. First the goat's milk was banished from the hospitals and regiments; then it was forbidden, and in Gibraltar the goats were themselves got rid of.

Results.—The prophylactic measures commenced in July 1906, and almost immediately a diminution of the disease occurred. Thus for the months of July, August, and September 1905 there were 258 cases; for the same months of 1906 there were only 26 cases.

In the Naval Hospital in Malta, a model institution in every respect previous to the stopping of the goats' milk, nearly every patient suffered from the disease; after stopping the supply of milk not a single case occurred.

From Gibraltar MAJOR HORROCKS reports the disappearance of Malta fever simultaneously with the disappearance of the Maltese goats.

CHAPTER VIII

THE RISE AND FALL OF DISEASE.—PLAGUE, TICK FEVER, LEPROSY AND TUBERCLE

RELAPSING FEVER (*SPIRILLOSIS*) AND PLAGUE

Plague.—The term " vermin fevers " might not inappropriately be given to the two diseases known respectively as *relapsing fever* and *plague*—two diseases as widely distributed over the globe as the vermin which have been proved to take a large share in their transmission. In their very wide distribution over the temperate and tropical zones they differ from yellow fever, malaria, and sleeping sickness, the insect carriers of which diseases flourish more vigorously in warm climates.

It is therefore not surprising that both these fevers have a world-wide distribution, as world-wide as the crawling and lively insects associated with them, namely, ticks and possibly bugs in the case of relapsing fever, and fleas in the case of plague. Nor is it surprising to find that both these diseases are being confined to diminishing areas of the globe. Time was when probably both had a far wider distribution than they have to-day. We know that

FIG. 44.—ORNITHO-
DOROS MOUBATA.
(Natural Size.)

The intermediary host of the
parasite which causes African
Relapsing Fever.

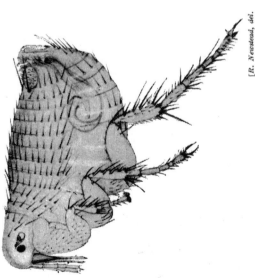

[R. Newstead, del.]

FIG. 43.—PLAGUE FLEA, LŒMOPSYLLA CHEOPIS, ROTHS.
(Greatly Enlarged.)

Europe was in the Middle Ages and even in later times devastated by epidemics of the plague or black death, the pestilence which wiped out entire populations and which we have every reason to believe was plague. To-day, the homes of plague have to be sought in the East and in India, to a less extent in Egypt; and it also bursts out sporadically in those parts of the world having intercourse with the East and which are not on the alert and are dirty, viz. the Pacific coast of the United States of America, and Australia, the Pacific seaboard of Central and South America, Mauritius, Madagascar, South-West Africa, South Africa, then finally the larger seaports in Europe.

If every now and then a few sporadic cases are found in Liverpool or Glasgow, or London, they are not feared, for they cannot spread, as the conditions for their spreading are not at hand; formerly they were, but now they have ceased to exist. Of course this is not the case in all parts of the world. Those places which have not come into line with these cities as regards modern hygiene are, as Europe was in the Middle Ages, still vulnerable. If we inquire into the reasons why plague has to so large a degree disappeared from countries where once it was pre- valent, and why to-day it is being confined to narrower areas, we must first recall what we have already learnt about malaria and yellow fever. We have seen how these diseases have steadily fallen back before improved water supplies and drainage—that is, before the destruction of the agents, the mosquitos, which propagate these diseases. Similarly with plague, the forces which have led to its extinction and curtailment are those grouped under Sanitary Reform—improved ways of living, less overcrowding, refuse removal and destruction, sewering and water supplies, better food, hospitals for the isolation of suspected cases, strict sanitary control by means of medical officers and sanitary inspectors ; these are the weapons of civilisation which have steadily driven back the agencies at work in transmitting plague. Now let us inquire what these agencies are. Plague is a disease caused by a bacillus, that is to say by a bacterial parasite or virus, and belongs to the class of diseases which also embraces typhoid, cholera, tubercle, leprosy. Like all the bacterial diseases, it may be transmitted in various ways, such as by direct contact, by contaminated food and clothing. But there is one special way by which we know it is spread, and that is why we discuss it here, namely by means of an insect,—in this case the flea. It has been shown by several observers, notably in 1906 by the investigations of the Plague Commission in India, that especially the rat flea, *Pulex cheopis*, acts as the carrier. It appears that when the flea takes up a meal of infected blood from a person suffering from plague, the bacilli are not killed in the body of the flea ; it has been shown that they even multiply ; when the infected flea bites a rat or a healthy human being it transmits the virus. The rat flea, it would appear therefore, is the chief transmitting agent, and this explains why the rat in common with man is the greatest sufferer from plague.

Epidemics of plague amongst rats often precede those
in man, and dead and sick rats have always been
regarded with the gravest suspicion in countries
liable to plague. These observations therefore teach
us that the rat and the particular flea which infests
it are the agents which must be regarded as largely
responsible for the spread of this disease. And, just
as in the case of the mosquito-borne diseases special
sanitary measures—the attack, in other words—must be
directed against them, so in plague in all anti-plague
measures a special war must be waged against the rat.
Anti-rat measures are enforced; steps are taken in all
epidemics to exterminate them both on ships and
in towns. Indeed as a precautionary measure in those
places where plague is liable to be introduced, the
rats are systematically examined throughout the year,
as in Liverpool, to try to detect at the earliest
possible stage an acutely or chronically infected rat.
The rats on ships coming from ports where plague is
known to exist are of course subjected to very special
bacteriological scrutiny; and as a further precaution
means are adopted to prevent the rats from such ships
getting on shore. By these means, if plague is
discovered in the rat the sanitary authority is fore-
warned, and is able to take effective steps before the
disease has attacked man. Again, just as in the case
of yellow fever and malaria the essential part of the
plan of campaign is to exterminate the anophelines and
the stegomyia, so, in the case of plague, the root of
prophylaxis is to exterminate the rat, and with it, its
own special flea which is the carrier. We see now,

moreover, how improved sanitation, better housing, prevention of overcrowding, sewering, and destruction of filth will diminish the natural hunting grounds of the rat, and therefore of its flea, and will in consequence lessen the chance of spreading the disease; and this is why plague has died out in places where hygiene is good and survives where there still exist overcrowding, squalor, and dirt.

TICK FEVER

This is the second of the diseases communicated by vermin. The name is of comparatively recent introduction, but the disease in some form has been known for many years. The relationship of ticks to the propagation of disease has been worked out most carefully in animals. Investigations by Drs. Smith, Kilborne, and Stiles in the United States showed that Texas cattle fever or red-water was spread from animal to animal by the bites of the ticks with which they were often covered. A tick bites an infected animal, and by so doing infects itself. In the case of the female tick the infection is passed on to the offspring, which, being infected, are capable of transmitting the virus to healthy beasts, and so the disease is spread.

As so often happens, that which occurs in the ·lower animals finds its parallel in man. And in effect, in 1904, two sets of investigators working independently in Africa proved that the well-known *spirillum* of relapsing fever, the parasite which sets up this disease in man, was transmitted from man to man by the bite of a tick, the *Ornithodoros moubata*, the disease induced receiving in consequence the name of Tick Fever.

Two of the investigators who had been sent out by the Liverpool School, Drs. Dutton and Todd, proved the further interesting facts, namely, that the parasite taken up by the parent tick in its meal of blood could pass into the egg and larva; in other words, could pass into the blood,—facts which Pasteur had shown to occur in the case of silkworm disease. The infected silkworm moth transmitted to the egg, and these to the worms which developed from them, the virus of that disease. So with these ticks. As the result of biting a man harbouring the parasite, they infected themselves and their offspring, thus producing a miniature epidemic amongst themselves and their offspring; and presumably these infected or diseased ticks are capable of communicating the parasite to man when they attack him. It was whilst engaged upon this research that Dr. Dutton lost his life by accidentally becoming infected with the disease.

It thus having been established that fleas can infect man with plague, and that ticks transmit the parasites of relapsing fever, it is not unreasonable to suppose that other crawling vermin can also take their part in the propagation of disease; hence the great importance of measures to ensure the cleanliness of the people, as, for example, by the anti-verminous Act. Insects that can pass from person to person are highly dangerous, and every endeavour should be made to get rid of them. Further, as we have evidence

15

that relapsing fever was once, like plague, a disease widely spread over the temperate as well as over the tropical zones, and as we know that it still persists in those districts where there is still overcrowding, so we must naturally come to the conclusion that this disease is dying out as the result of civilisation and its attendant sanitary reforms. It is, like plague and yellow fever, being chased out of the world or confined to smaller and smaller areas. What has been accomplished in the case of relapsing fever and plague should encourage man to redouble his energies to finally stamp out yellow fever, malaria, and plague, more especially now, as there is no excuse for their existence seeing that we know precisely how to attack them. In addition to the methods of general sanitation, we have now specific weapons, and the world should not rest content until these diseases are absolutely eradicated.

These are not theoretical considerations; they are eminently practical, as the history of the rise and fall of disease has proved to us. To recapitulate, we stated how only fifty years ago the mortality from yellow fever in the West Indies reached 69 per cent. amongst our garrisons. Plague was once the pestilence of Europe. Cholera once swept over Europe and many parts of the world. Small-pox was once much more deadly and common; so common, in fact, that it was regarded as the right thing to get it and have done with it, just as often the planter to-day regards malaria. Clearly the victory is on our side, and we must push it home.

A very fascinating object-lesson is furnished by the struggle between man and disease, and it is this. We are apt to regard the virus or germs of disease as a dead chemical and poisonous substance, a substance which having been introduced into our system will have to run itself out, during which process we may or may not survive. The study of the tropical diseases reveals to us the fact that the causes of the diseases are organised living elements—we term them parasites—which are struggling for an existence in our bodies and those of animals; like all other species of living matter, they only want to live. When man, however, finds out that this living is done at his expense, in the shape of loss of health and very often death, he bestirs himself against these competitors. He has to adopt every means in his power to ward them off, for he is now aware that these living parasites in his blood or intestines are equally struggling to survive in our bodies, and when we use one method of defence they in their turn harden themselves to withstand it. This is seen, for example, in the gradually increasing resistance which the parasites of malaria and sleeping sickness offer respectively to quinine and arsenic. When these drugs are first administered they are much more efficacious, that is to say, they kill more parasites; later the parasites develop natural resisting powers and are less affected. The struggle therefore resolves itself into a deliberate contest for supremacy in the animal kingdom between the highest and the lowest representatives. This consideration should still further fortify us to continue the fight.

LEPROSY AND TUBERCULOSIS

Just as tick fever or plague teaches us a very significant lesson as regards the rise and fall of disease in the history of mankind, so to-day the bacterial diseases known by the respective names of leprosy and tuberculosis also give us very much cause for reflection.

Leprosy is a very widely distributed disease. It can still be seen in its most flourishing condition in the tropics, but it is by no means limited to the warmer latitudes; there is much of it still in the north of Europe. And we must all be familiar with the fact that formerly it was not only very prevalent in Europe, but even in this country. The precise manner in which it is transmitted from person to person is not known. Numerous theories to account for its spread have been from time to time propounded, but they are none of them satisfactory. Beauperthuy, who had a very considerable experience of the disease, regarded the insect vermin *Sarcoptes scabeii* as taking a very leading share in its transmission; he also viewed with suspicion the house fly. It is a fact that the sarcoptes is very frequently associated with leprosy; and, just as in the case of the tick- and flea-carried diseases, there may be some intimate relationship. But the great lesson which leprosy teaches us is the magnificent results which sanitation and the skilled care of the sick can bring about. The leper no longer roams about or is allowed to rot in some disused hut little better than a dog-kennel. He is taken and cared for in beautifully

kept hospitals and lazarettos, where he is well fed
and his existence made tolerable; and those of
us who have seen him in these institutions will, I
am sure, agree that a great debt of gratitude is due
to those devoted nurses and to the sisterhoods who
devote their lives to his care: they are helping in
an unmistakable way to make the world healthier,
and it is one of the great reasons why this terrible
disease is becoming less.

While leprosy is diminishing, an allied disease, often
called the white man's plague, appears to be spreading
in the tropical world. The cause is probably not very
far to seek. We know that the wild animals are not
prone to this disease, but the domestic animals are.
Similarly, we have reason to believe that the wild man
is less prone than the civilised man to contract the
disease. When, however, with the extension of commerce, the native races begin to copy more and more
our ways of living, they render themselves equally
liable to our diseases. We have already pointed out
how the domestic animals share with us diseases in
common. The native, instead of living as of old in his
freer and less crowded state, comes into the larger
villages and towns to seek work; overcrowding in consequence results, too many live huddled together in one
room and with hardly any ventilation. The consequence
is that if tubercle is once introduced, it tends to spread
and to infect the floors and walls of the living rooms.
No wonder then that the question of tuberculosis is
giving much cause for anxiety in some of our tropical
possessions, for no doubt history will repeat itself, and,

just as we have witnessed the spread of consumption in this country and have taken energetic measures to stop it, so with tropical countries and with crowded populations the disease will spread and most energetic measures will have to be adopted to stem it. Tuberculosis is not the only white man's disease which shows signs of increase; there are also others. Thus we are brought face to face with the curious fact that whilst man is steadily stamping out certain diseases which for the most part interfere with his commerce, there are a few diseases associated more especially with his comparatively luxurious way of living which are not kept under and are especially apt to spread quickly amongst the native races who come in contact with us and copy our methods.

APPENDIX

ANTILARVAL AND DRAINAGE REGULATIONS, ORDI-
NANCES, AND BYE-LAWS, RAT AND PLAGUE
REGULATIONS, IN TRINIDAD, BRITISH GUIANA,
BARBADOS, ST. VINCENT, ST. LUCIA, GRENADA,
NASSAU, MAURITIUS, SIERRA LEONE, SAN FRANCISCO

EXPEDITIONS AND COMMISSIONS SENT TO THE TROPICS
BY THE ROYAL SOCIETY AND THE LIVERPOOL AND
LONDON SCHOOLS OF TROPICAL MEDICINE

TRINIDAD

In March 1907 Regulations were made under Section 8 of
Ordinance 188 to deal with yellow fever by screening patients,
fumigation, etc., and by prohibiting the keeping of stagnant
water, unless properly protected. It runs as follows:

(a) No water shall be stored (except in small quantities
for drinking purposes) unless efficiently protected against
mosquitos by the following method :
All tanks, barrels, etc., for storing water shall have
all openings except the draw-off opening covered with
wire-gauze (18 mesh to the inch), or with a piece of cheese
cloth or fine mosquito netting, and all fountains, pools,
ponds, antiformicas or excavations made for any purpose
whatever, in public or private property, which may
contain water, shall be kept stocked with mosquito-
destroying fish, or shall be kept covered with a film of
petroleum oil.

(b) The occupier or owner of any premises shall keep such
premises free of stagnant water, liable to breed mosquitos,

and the presence of mosquito larvæ in any collection of water, wherever situated, shall be sufficient evidence that such water is stagnant.

(c) The occupier or owner of any premises shall keep his premises free of all articles (bottles whole or broken, old tins, boxes, conch shell, etc.) which may retain water and so become the breeding places of mosquitos.

(d) All watery cess-pits shall be disinfected or oiled and all catch-pits cleaned out at least once a week.

(e) All eaves-gutters and down-pipes shall be maintained in good repair and free of obstruction so as to allow the ready passage of water from the roofs of houses.

(f) The Medical Officer of Health or any person authorised by him in writing shall have authority to enter any premises at any time between the hours of 6 a.m. and 8 p.m. for the purpose of seeing that these regulations are carried out.

6. Any person failing to comply with these regulations shall be guilty of an offence and be liable to a fine not exceeding twenty pounds.

In the new draft Ordinance for 1909 provisions similar to the above are inserted for dealing with the breeding places of mosquitos.

In March 1909 a leaflet was widely distributed by the Surgeon-General repeating these clauses and emphasising the £20 penalty. Action was taken and many fines inflicted.

On January 16, 1908, additional regulations were passed dealing with " Contacts," and a Report published as follows :

The regulations of the 22nd March and 6th April, 1907, were revised, provisions for dealing with " Contacts " were added and the whole were consolidated—passed by the Governor in Council on the 16th January, 1908, and published in the *Royal Gazette*.

In each case of yellow fever occurring in Port-of-Spain a large area surrounding the infected house was promptly defined and every house and yard within such area was rapidly subjected to a rigid inspection and cleansing, special attention being devoted to actual and potential breeding places of mosquitos.

A portable and readily adaptable apparatus for screening yellow fever patients was devised and used when required. Isolation was maintained in each case at the patient's residence. The number of these was reduced as circumstances permitted, and they were dispensed with altogether for a short period, four being re-employed between 1st January and 7th March.

The numbers were gradually reduced and the brigade was disbanded towards the end of November 1907. It was again brought into operation on the 6th January, and has since been employed in reduced number. Every building in which a case of yellow fever occurred was thoroughly fumigated—including all outbuildings within the same curtilage, and adjacent premises when necessary ; twenty-nine premises were dealt with, including the convents of St. Joseph and Holy Name.

ST. LUCIA

Shortly after his arrival in 1905 Administrator P. Cork directed the attention of the Sanitary Officers to the importance of the destruction of the breeding places of mosquitos in towns and villages, and gave special instructions to the police on the subject.

In November 1905 the Administrator, P. Cork, wrote to the Inspector of Prisons.

A circular was also directed by the Administrator in November 1905 to all Medical Officers.

A Police Order, dated November 1905, was also issued :

CIRCULAR TO MEDICAL OFFICERS

GOVERNMENT OFFICE
November 25, 1905

Being desirous of obtaining reliable information as to the prevalence of mosquito-borne diseases in this Colony, I shall feel very much obliged if you will be so good as to favour me with a return showing the number and description of such disease which may have come under your notice either in your public capacity or in your private practice during the past twelve months.

2. If convenient to you to add particulars of any other preventible disease which may be prevalent I shall be much obliged.

THE FOLLOWING USEFUL NOTICE HAS RECENTLY BEEN
ISSUED TO HOUSEHOLDERS IN ST. LUCIA

1. In the general interest of the public health and particularly to prevent the introduction and spread of yellow fever which

would most seriously affect the trade of the island, every householder is invited to co-operate with the Health Authorities in the destruction of mosquitos.

2. It is by mosquitos that both yellow fever and the ordinary malarial fever are carried and spread.

3. Mosquitos can only breed in stagnant water, therefore you are requested to see that—

(a) Any tanks or jars or other water receptacles in your yard are screened according to the Board of Health Regulations, to prevent mosquitos getting into the water to breed.

> N.B.—The Health Authorities will be prepared to examine premises and give advice as to the proper way of screening, etc. In Castries a specimen of such screening can be seen at the Police Station.

(b) All wells are filled up.

> N.B.—Well water in Castries is most unwholesome.

(c) That none of the following articles are kept lying about your yard or lots .

  i. Bottles : whole or broken,
  ii. Tins,
  iii. Broken pieces of earthenware,
  iv. Coco-nuts,
  v. Calabashes,

or any other thing capable of holding water.

(d) That all hollows in the ground about your yards or adjacent premises are filled up to the level, so that water may not collect in them.

(e) That water kept in—

  i. Washing-tubs,
  ii. Flower vases,
  iii. Chickens' drinking vessels

is changed very frequently and the vessels *kept free from moss*, because the green moss found in such vessels harbours the mosquito larvæ and keeps them alive while the water is being changed.

Issued by advice of the Medical Board.

H. A. SMALLWOOD,
Acting Colonial Secretary.

July 7, 1909.

GRENADA

Under the Public Health Ordinances 1902 and 1905, regulations were made April 24, 1907, to deal with yellow fever from the point of view of reporting suspects, fumigation and antilarval measures It runs as follows :—

YELLOW FEVER

1. A Medical Officer upon becoming aware *or on suspecting* that any person in his district is suffering from Yellow Fever shall, if he has not already done so, visit such person without delay and report the facts to the Local Sanitary Authority of his district, as well as to the General Board of Health through Colonial Secretary as required by section 4 of Ordinance No. 13 of 1905.

2. Where the patient is found or suspected on such visit to be suffering from Yellow Fever the Medical Officer shall forthwith cause him to be placed under a mosquito net, and may direct him to be isolated in an apartment or building so screened as to effectually prevent the access of mosquitos thereto, and it shall be the duty of the occupier of such premises to carefully cause such screens to be kept closed.

3. Where the patient aforesaid is ordered by the proper authority to be removed to an Isolation Station or Hospital, he shall only be so removed in an ambulance or vehicle which is effectually screened against mosquitos, and it shall be the duty of the person in charge of such ambulance or vehicle to see that such screen is not opened unnecessarily. Any such Isolation Station or Hospital shall be so screened as to effectually prevent the access of mosquitos thereto.

4. Where any house or building or any part thereof in which any case of Yellow Fever or suspected case of Yellow Fever has occurred is ordered to be cleansed and disinfected (under the authority of section 8 of Ordinance No. 13 of 1905) such operation shall include its fumigation to the satisfaction of the Medical Officer and so as to effectually destroy any mosquitos therein.

5. Immediately upon any case of Yellow Fever being reported in any place in a district, the Local Sanitary Authority shall cause regular house-to-house visitation to be made in the vicinity of such place to ascertain whether any other cases of fever have occurred; and the district Medical Officer shall assist the Local Sanitary Authority and its inspectors in such visitation, and they are hereby empowered to strictly enforce the following measures for the eradication of mosquitos in such place and its neighbourhood:

(a) No water shall be stored (except in small quantities for drinking purposes) unless efficiently protected against mosquitos by the following method :

All tanks, barrels, etc., for storing water shall have all

openings except the draw-off opening covered with wire gauze (18 mesh to the inch), or with a piece of cheese cloth, and all fountains, pools, ponds, or excavations, made for any purpose whatever, in public or private property, which may contain water, shall be kept stocked with mosquito-destroying fish, or shall be kept covered with a film of petroleum.

(b) The occupier or owner of any premises shall keep such premises free of stagnant water, liable to breed mosquitos, and the presence of mosquito larvæ in any collection of water, wherever situated, shall be sufficient evidence that such water is stagnant.

(c) The occupier or owner of any premises shall keep his premises free of all articles (bottles whole or broken, old tins, boxes, conch shells, &c.) which may contain water and so become the breeding places of mosquitos, including broken bottles on walls.

(d) All watery cess-pits shall be disinfected or oiled and all catch-pits cleaned out at least once a week.

(e) All eaves-gutters and down-pipes shall be maintained in good repair and free of obstruction so as to allow the ready passage of water from the roofs of houses.

(f) The District Medical Officer or any person authorised by him in writing shall have authority to enter any premises at any time between the hours of 6 a.m. and 8 p.m. for the purpose of seeing that these Regulations are carried out.

On August 30, 1907, a further notice was issued entitled :

REGULATION FOR THE PREVENTION OF YELLOW FEVER

The Regulation No. 4, passed by the General Board of Health, on April 24, 1907, is hereby rescinded, and the following regulation is made in its place.

4. Where any house or building or any part thereof is, in consequence of the occurrence of any case of Yellow Fever, or suspected case of Yellow Fever, ordered to be cleansed and disinfected (under the authority of section 8 of Ordinance No. 13 of 1905) such operation shall include its fumigation to the satisfaction of the Medical Officer, and so as to effectually destroy any mosquitos therein, as well as the fumigation in like manner of such of the houses or buildings in the immediate neighbourhood thereof, as the said Medical Officer may certify in writing to be

necessary with a view to the destruction of possibly infected mosquitos.

Approved and passed by the General Board of Health this 30th day of August, 1907.

Since my visit (May 1909) most useful regulations dealing with mosquito larvæ have been passed, as follows :

PUBLIC HEALTH ORDINANCES, 1902 AND 1905

REGULATIONS FOR DECLARING THE BREEDING PLACES OF MOS-QUITOS, IN AND ABOUT HUMAN HABITATIONS, TO BE STATUTORY NUISANCES

Under and by virtue of sections 11 and 23 of the Public Health Ordinance 1902, the General Board of Health hereby declares the following matters to be deemed nuisances liable at all times to be dealt with summarily under the provisions of the said Ordinance :

1. Any accumulation of any stagnant water in any town or in or about any human habitation, which accumulation results from want of proper care or from want of repair to any construction or defective construction.

2. Any articles or receptacles or any construction holding stagnant water, not being a receptacle or construction designed and used for the storage of water.

3. Any receptacle or construction, designed and used for the storage of water, which is not either—
   (i) cleared or emptied daily, or
   (ii) effectively screened, from the access thereto by mosquitos, with wire-gauze (18 mesh, at least, to the inch) or, in the case of receptacles kept in the house, with a covering of cheese cloth, or
   (iii) stocked with mosquito-destroying fish, or
   (iv) covered with a film of oil.

4. Any pond or pit containing water, situate in a town, or within 150 yards of a human habitation, which is not stocked with mosquito-destroying fish or covered with a film of oil.

5. Any receptacle used for storing water, which receptacle may have been condemned as unnecessary under notice in writing of the local sanitary authority served or left on any premises in pursuance of the provisions of any Regulations made under the authority of section 20 of Ordinance No. 13 of 1905.

And it is hereby declared that any collection of water shall for the purposes of these Regulations be regarded as "stagnant water" if the same contains mosquito larvæ or if the same has been left undisturbed for a period exceeding 18 hours.

Made by the General Board of Health this 21st day of June, 1909.

By order of the Board,
T. T. DYER.
Clerk to General Board of Health.

Also a most useful Ordinance for the destruction of rats:

THE RATS ORDINANCE, 1909

REGULATIONS FOR THE DESTRUCTION OF RATS, ETC., ON VESSELS

1. Any Medical Officer, on becoming aware or upon suspecting that any vessel lying within any waters of the Colony is infested with rats or other vermin, is hereby empowered to strictly enforce the adoption of such measures as may in his discretion be deemed most efficacious for the purposes of exterminating the said rats or vermin and of preventing such rats or vermin passing from such vessel to the shore or from the shore to such vessel. Such measures may include the following:

(*a*) Require the owner, master or person in charge of the vessel, when at any mooring or when loading or unloading cargo at any port within the Colony, to use rat-guards of a pattern approved by the said Officer on every rope, cable or such-like communication passing between such vessel and the shore or between the vessel and any lighter or barge or other vessel, or between the vessel and its buoys or anchors or the mooring.

(*b*) Require the owner, master or person in charge to generally abate all insanitary conditions where they exist, and to effectually remove or burn all rubbish and deposits on the vessel likely to harbour rats or vermin.

(*c*) Whenever it shall appear to the Medical Officer that the rats or vermin can only be exterminated by cleansing and disinfection in a specified manner, the Medical Officer may, by notice in writing, either require the owner, master or person in charge of the vessel to cleanse and disinfect or fumigate the same accordingly, or may inform such owner, master or person that it is the intention of the Medical Officer to conduct such cleansing and disinfection or fumigation at a time to be specified in the notice.

2. Where the owner, master or person in charge of such vessel

fails to comply with any requirements made under these Regulations, or is, from poverty or otherwise, unable to effectually carry out such requirements, the Medical Officer may cause the requisite measures to be taken forthwith, and the expenses thereby incurred may, at the discretion of the General Board of Health, be either defrayed from General Revenue, or be recovered wholly, or in part, from such owner, master, or person.

3. It shall be the duty of all Port, Revenue, and Police Officers to assist the Medical Officers in enforcing the provision of, and preventing any infringement of, these Regulations.

4. Any person acting in violation of these Regulations, either by way of refusing to obey any requisition or instruction, made or given hereunder, or by obstructing in any way the due execution of these Regulations, renders himself liable to a fine not exceeding twenty pounds.

Made by the Governor in Council this 21st day of June, 1909.

T. T. DYER.
Clerk of Council.

ST. VINCENT

The Public Health Act of 1865 naturally contained no anti-mosquito regulations.

Therefore an ordinance (No. 3, 1901) was passed to repeal it, and under this ordinance Regulations were made in 1907 to deal according to modern methods with yellow fever and mosquitos as follows :

THE PUBLIC HEALTH ORDINANCE, 1901

REGULATIONS MADE BY THE GOVERNOR IN COUNCIL UNDER THE
AUTHORITY OF SECTION 20

1. When disinfection of any house or premises is ordered or effected under Regulations 8–11 of the Public Health Regulations of the 16th March, 1903, such disinfection may include fumigation to the satisfaction of the Government Medical Officer so as to effectually destroy any mosquitos therein.

2. The provisions contained in Regulations 14 and 15 of the Public Health Regulations of the 16th March, 1903, as to isolation and removal of persons suffering from infectious or contagious disease shall, notwithstanding anything contained in the Public Health Regulations of the 23rd July, 1903, apply where any

Government Medical Officer suspects that any person is or may be suffering from Yellow Fever.

3. The occupier of any premises in any town, or in case of their being no person in occupation, the owner thereof, shall keep the premises free from stagnant water likely to breed mosquitos, and the presence of mosquito larvæ in any collection of water shall be sufficient evidence that such water is stagnant; and he shall also keep the premises free from tins, bottles, whole or broken (including broken bottles on walls), tubs, barrels, odd receptacles, broken crockery, etc., kept or left in a position likely to accumulate and retain water and so become breeding places for mosquitos.

4. Immediately upon any case of Yellow Fever or suspected Yellow Fever being reported, the Local Authority or Local Authorities for the district or districts in or near to which the case has occurred shall make or cause to be made regular house-to-house visitation in their district in the vicinity of such place to ascertain whether any other cases of fever have occurred, and the Government Medical Officer of the district shall assist the Local Authority by examining any person the Local Authority may require, and the Local Authority shall see that, in any town, the provisions of the last preceding Regulation have been, and are, observed, and shall also have power and authority to order and direct the owner or occupier of any premises in the neighbourhood of which any such case has occurred, and whether the premises be, or be not in any town, for a period of not exceeding three months from such order and direction :

(a) To comply with the requirements of the last preceding Regulation.

(b) To cover all openings except the draw-off opening in tanks, barrels, etc., used for storing water, with wire-gauze (not less than in 18 mesh to the inch), or with a piece of cheese cloth.

(c) To either cover and keep covered with a film of kerosene oil, or draw off and keep drawn off, or fill up, all pools, ponds or excavations made for any purpose, which may contain water.

(d) To disinfect in manner directed, or to oil once a week any watery cess-pit, and to flush out or clean at least once a week any drain, or gutter.

(e) To repair and free from obstruction any eaves-gutters and down-pipes and to keep the same repaired and freed from obstruction so as to allow the free passage of water from the roofs of houses.

All persons shall comply with the orders or directions of the

Local Authority, or of any inspector authorised by them in writing, in respect of any of the above matters.'

5. The Local Authority or any person authorised in writing by the Local Authority is hereby empowered to enter any premises at any time between the hours of 6 a.m. and 6 p.m. for the purpose of enforcing the provisions of these Regulations.

Made by the Governor in Council this 8th day of May, 1907.

V. F. DRAYTON,
Acting Clerk of Council.

N.B.—By the provisions of Section 21 of the Public Health Ordinance 1901, any person who—

1. Violates these regulations : or
2. Refuses or neglects to obey the same ; or
3. Resists, opposes, or obstructs the lawful execution thereof,

—is liable to a penalty not exceeding twenty pounds or to imprisonment with or without hard labour for any period not exceeding six months.

This year (1909) a new Bill is being prepared, to be called the Public Health Ordinance 1909, containing provisions against stagnant water and mosquito larvæ. Provision is made for bringing water under proper control and supervision, etc.

BRITISH GUIANA

The old Public Health Act not containing any reference to antimosquito measures, special bye-laws were enacted..

In 1905 a bye-law for the cleansing of tanks without, however, special reference to larvæ, was issued.

In 1907 bye-laws relating to the screening of vats, etc., as a preventive against mosquitos were promulgated under the title " Mosquito Prevention Bye-Laws, 1907," as follows :

BYE-LAWS RELATING TO THE SCREENING OF VATS, ETC., AS A PREVENTIVE AGAINST MOSQUITOS

1. These bye-laws may be cited as the Mosquito Prevention Bye-Laws, 1907.

2. All vats, tanks, or other vessels shall be screened with mosquito-proof wire-netting or other suitable material so as to prevent the entrance into or exit of mosquitos from such vats or tanks or other vessels.

16

3. The inlet and overflow pipes into such vats, tanks or other vessels shall be placed in such positions or screened in such a manner as to prevent the entrance into or exit from the same of mosquitos.

4. All buckets or other vessels containing water for fire-extinguishing or other purposes shall be emptied and cleansed at least once a week.

5. The work of screening the vats, tanks, and all such other vessels shall be done by the owners of the properties on which they are situated, and all vats, tanks, or other vessels shall be screened within three months from the date of the coming into force of these bye-laws.

6. Any person contravening any of these bye-laws shall be guilty of an offence, and on summary conviction, be liable to a penalty not exceeding ten dollars.

Made by the Mayor and Town Council of Georgetown under Section 179 of the Local Government Ordinance, 1907, and confirmed by the Governor and Court of Policy on the second day of September, 1907.

These do not appear, owing to considerable prejudice, to have been enforced. I had, however, the opportunity of discussing them with the Mayor and Town Council, with the result as follows :

PUBLIC NOTICE

VAT SCREENING

THE Mayor and Town Council having directed that the Vat Screening Regulations of 1907 are in future to be rigidly enforced, and the Sanitary Inspectors of the several Wards having been instructed to notify property owners and householders accordingly, public notice is hereby given that all persons failing by the 15th July next to comply with such Regulations in respect to the efficient screening of tanks, vats, barrels, and other vessels used for the storage of water, will be proceeded against as the law directs.

Advice as to the best methods of screening to be adopted will be given when required on application at my office.

By order of the Mayor and Town Council.

LUKE M. HILL,
Town Superintendent.

TOWN HALL, GEORGETOWN,
June 8, 1909.

VAT SCREENING IN GEORGETOWN

Sir,—In reference to your paragraph in this morning's issue about vat screening in Georgetown, I may mention for the information of the public that *many hundred* vats have already been screened, notwithstanding your statement that only " *a comparatively small number* " have been so treated.

It may be of some interest to those property owners still in default to know that the following general order to Town Overseers was issued by me on Thursday :

" As the days of grace allowed for vat screening expire to-day, I shall be glad if the overseers will make out a return of all vats screened and unscreened in their respective districts with a view of instituting some prosecutions of recalcitrant owners and occupiers, as an example to others ; and to show that it is intended to enforce the vat screening regulations.

" I expect these returns to be made from *personal inspections* of the storage vessels, and not from casual inquiries made from the householders."—I am, sir, etc.,

LUKE M. HILL,
Town Superintendent.

TOWN HALL,
July 16, 1909.

By Ordinance 13, 1907, stress had been laid upon the necessity of drainage. The bye-Laws are as follows :

DRAINAGE BYE-LAWS

FOR THE CITY OF GEORGETOWN, IN THE COUNTY OF DEMERARA, COLONY OF BRITISH GUIANA, WITH RESPECT TO THE DRAINAGE OF LOTS

MEMORANDUM

THE PUBLIC HEALTH ORDINANCE, 1878 (NOW LOCAL GOVERNMENT ORDINANCE No. 13, 1907), ENACTS :

23. (174, new Ordinance 13, 1907.) The owner or, when required by the local authority, the occupier of every lot of land situate in a Town or Village district shall effectually drain the lot, and for that purpose shall :

1. Make such dams and drains on the lot as may be necessary for effectually draining the lot ;
2. Fill up all irregularities in the surface of the lot ; and
3. Adjust the surface thereof, and if necessary raise the level of the surface thereof, in such a manner—

(*a*) That the water received on the lot may flow into the drains without obstruction ;

(*b*) That no water can remain on any portion of the surface of the lot other than the drains ; and

(*c*) That the surface of the lot does not remain swampy.

Provided that where the swampy state of any lot in any such district is occasioned by the main drains into which the drains of the lot discharge not having a sufficient outfall·or a sufficient capacity to carry off all the water discharged into them, the owner or occupier of the lot shall not be liable under this section to raise the level of the surface of the lot if the level of such surface is as high as the average height of the level of the land surrounding such a lot for a distance of twenty roods ; and

Provided that any owner may, with the consent of the local authority of the district in which the lot is situate, have a pond on the lot.

24. (175, new Ordinance 13, of 1907.) Every local authority may make bye-laws :

1. For regulating the number, position, length, and width of all drains, the materials of which they are to be constructed, the mode of their construction, and the main drains into which they are to discharge ;

2. For imposing on the owner of the lot, or on the occupier, or on each occupier of the lot or of any building thereon, the duty of keeping the drains on or adjoining the lot clean and wholesome and free from obstruction ;

3. For determining in what cases there is to be one drain common to two adjoining lots and how the expense of the same is to be divided between the owners or occupiers of such lots ; and such bye-laws may apply to the whole or any specified part of the district of such local authority.

26. (New Ordinance 176.) Where any lot within a town or village district is not effectually drained . . . the local authority shall, by a written notice, require in the first case the owner or occupier of the lot or of any building on the lot, and in the second case the owner or occupier of the land or of the dwelling-house thereon, or if there be more than one of such owners or occupiers, then any one or more of such owners or occupiers, to perform within a reasonable time to be specified in the notice all or any of the obligations imposed by this Ordinance on the owner or occupier for effectually draining the lot or portion of the land.

If any owner or occupier fails to perform any act required by such notice to be performed he shall be liable to a penalty not exceeding twenty-four dollars, and to a further penalty not exceeding three dollars for each day during which such failure shall continue after the expiration of the time specified in the notice.

Where the notice is not complied with (and notwithstanding proceedings may have been or are about to be instituted for the recovery of the penalty for non-compliance therewith) the local authority may, after the expiration of the time specified in the notice, do the work required, and may recover in a summary manner the expenses incurred by them in so doing from the owner or occupier of the lot in the first case, and in the second case from the owner or occupier of the land or the dwelling-house thereon, or may by order declare the same to be private improvement expenses.

Any expense incurred by the occupier of any lot or building in complying with any notice under this section may be recovered by him from the owner of the lot or of the land on which the building is erected, unless the necessity for the work required by the said notice to be performed was rendered necessary by the act of the occupier, or unless it has been otherwise agreed between the owner and occupier.

AS TO DRAINAGE.

1. Every lot exceeding fifty feet in width shall have not less than two drains, and every lot under and not up to fifty feet in width shall have at least one drain.

2. Each such drain shall be so placed:

(a) That the centre thereof shall not be less than two feet from the nearest boundary line of the lot unless the Town Superintendent, the circumstances being exceptional, shall give permission in writing to place any such drain nearer to such boundary line;

(b) That such drains shall run clear from and outside of all buildings on the lot in a straight line without any bend or angle unless the Town Superintendent, the circumstances being exceptional, shall give permission in writing to place any such bend or angle in any such drain;

(c) That the tops of the sides of such drain shall be below the level of the surface of the lot and that the said sides shall be pierced at intervals of not less than ten feet with holes of not less than one square inch in area, and being not less than two inches above the level of the bottom of the drain;

(d) That the bottom of such drain shall at the upper end or highest level thereof have a depth of not less than six inches, and shall have a fall towards the point of discharge of not less than two inches in every one hundred feet;

(c) That such drain shall discharge into the main drain in rear of the lot in all cases where such back drainage is provided , in all other cases, into the nearest main drain provided by the local authority for the reception of the lot-drainage of the district, and every question as to which is such nearest main drain shall be determined by the Town Superintendent.

3. Each such drain shall run through the lot from end to end or from side to side as may be necessary, having reference to the position of the main drain unless the Town Superintendent, the circumstances being exceptional, shall give permission in writing to construct any such drain for a shorter distance.

4. Each such drain shall have an internal width of not less than nine inches at the top and six at the bottom.

5. Each such drain shall be constructed of stone, brick, concrete, hardwood, or other suitable material, and in such manner as the Town Superintendent shall approve.

6. The drains on or adjoining any lot shall be kept clean and wholesome, and free from obstruction by the parties hereinafter named :

(a) The owner or, where there are more than one, each owner of the lot.

(b) The occupier of the lot or, where there are more occupiers than one, by each occupier.

(c) The occupier of any building on the lot.

7. The owner or owners of two adjoining lots may, having first obtained the permission in writing of the Town Superintendent, construct one drain common to such two adjoining lots.

8. Every such common drain shall be of not less than one and a half times the width required by these bye-laws for the drain of a single lot.

9. The expense of constructing any such common drain shall be divided between, and be payable in equal proportions by the owners of the lots drained thereby unless the Town Authority shall otherwise order in cases where the special circumstances show that one owner ought justly to pay more than the other.

10. If in the opinion of the Town Superintendent it is necessary for the efficient drainage of a lot that the drainage shall pass through or over an adjoining lot, the drains carrying off such drainage shall whenever practicable be made to pass through the side drains of the said adjoining lot hereinbefore provided for, and, if not so practicable, then such drainage shall be carried across such adjoining lot by means of a tunnel or covered drain of sufficient capacity constructed to the satisfaction of the Town

Superintendent as regards position, size and material, and the expense of constructing such tunnel or covered drain and of replacing the surface earth shall be borne wholly by the owner or owners of the lot from which the drainage comes.

11. If the Town Superintendent certifies that on the coming into operation of these bye-laws any lot is or was sufficiently drained, these bye-laws shall not be taken or held to require the construction of new drains on such lot, unless the drainage of the lot subsequently becomes defective or insufficient.

12. Efficient subsoil drainage, to the satisfaction of the Town Superintendent, may be permitted in lieu of the drains described in Bye-laws 2, 3 and 4.

13. The owner of any lot feeling aggrieved by the action of the Town Superintendent in any manner by these Bye-laws left to his decision may appeal to the Town Authority, whose decision shall be final.

14. Every person who shall offend against any of these bye-laws shall be liable for every such offence to a penalty of twenty-four dollars, and in the case of a continuing offence to a further penalty of three dollars for each day after written notice of the offence ·from the Town Authority:

Provided nevertheless that the magistrate, before whom any complaint may be made or any proceedings may be taken in respect of any such offence, may, if he think fit, adjudge the payment as a penalty of any sum less than the full amount of the penalty imposed by this bye-law.

BARBADOS

The Public Health Act of 1898, Section 8, contained some up-to-date regulations for the destruction of mosquitos. Good as they were, they were not, unfortunately, rigorously enforced.

2. The occupier or owner of any premises shall keep such premises free of stagnant water, liable to breed mosquitos, and the presence of mosquito larvæ in any collection of water, wherever situated, shall be sufficient evidence that such water is stagnant. All tanks, fountains, pools, ponds, or excavations made for any purpose whatever, in public or private property, which may contain water, shall be kept stocked with mosquito-destroying fish, or shall be kept covered with a film of petroleum oil.

3. The occupier or owner of any premises shall keep his premises free of all articles (bottles whole or broken, old tins, boxes, conch shells, etc.) which may retain water and so become the breeding places of mosquitos.

4. All cess-pits which retain water shall be disinfected or oiled except they be efficiently covered and trapped.

5. All gutters and down-pipes shall be maintained in good repair and free of obstruction so as to prevent the accumulation of water therein and to allow the ready passage of water from the roofs of houses.

6. All Inspectors of Health shall have authority to enter any premises at any time between the hours of 7 a.m. to 6 p.m. for the purpose of seeing that these Regulations are carried out, and may pour oil or cause oil to be poured on the surface of water contained in any receptacle in or on such premises.

Made by the General Board of Health this 22nd day of February, 1909.

President.

Confirmed by the Governor in Executive Committee this day of February, 1909.

Colonial Secretary.

When the epidemic broke out a manifesto was issued by the President of the Board of Health, Dr. Chandler, to Commissioners and Inspectors of Health, etc. :

SIR,

Yellow Fever is spreading in various parts of the Island.

There are two points whose importance you probably realise already but which cannot be too frequently impressed on every Commissioner of Health and every Inspector of Health in view of the grave danger resulting from a want of their proper consideration.

1. It is during the first three days of illness that the Yellow Fever patient infects mosquitos, and every such patient who remains unscreened from mosquitos during the whole or a material part of these three days if bitten by Stegomyia mosquitos, which abound in Barbados, makes his place of abode the centre of a new Yellow Fever infected district.

Our recent experience has clearly demonstrated that in many cases it is difficult for the attendant medical practitioner to diagnose Yellow Fever in the earlier stage of the disease.

The returns made of the cases that have occurred during the present epidemic show that a large number of cases have only been seen for the first time by a medical man after the expiration of the first three days of the disease. With this result of the present state of things its continuation can only mean the spread of the epidemic.

To prevent this spread steps must be taken to ensure as far as possible that every Yellow Fever patient be screened from mosquitos during the first three days of his illness.

To effect this every person suffering from fever of any sort should as a matter of precaution be screened from mosquitos as soon as possible after the development of fever. Patients of the labouring classes are not in ordinary circumstances seen by a medical man until some time after the occurrence of fever.

To cope with the existing situation there must be a daily house-to-house inquiry as to the health of inmates not likely to summon a medical man on the first appearance of illness, prompt attendance by a medical man at the public expense on every person having fever of any sort, and proper arrangements for immediately carrying out at the public expense every direction by a medical man to screen a patient from mosquitos.

2. The destruction of the largest possible number of mosquitos which have had the opportunity of coming into contact with a Yellow Fever patient is most essential.

A mosquito infected with Yellow Fever can live and infect persons with that disease for many months.

In the returns made to the Board of Health by Sanitary Inspectors they invariably report that they have "disinfected and fumigated," and the result of inquiries made show that in many cases these words correctly describe the order of procedure adopted.

Some Inspectors in their use of disinfectant do everything possible to chase the mosquitos out of the infected premises, and having done this more or less effectively then proceed to close up the premises and fumigate for the destruction of mosquitos.

One can scarcely imagine any mode of procedure which would tend more to the spread of the epidemic.

Similar directions were placarded in all prominent places throughout the town and many districts.

At the same time also a large number of handbills were printed warning householders against the danger of keeping stagnant water, and the penalties for the same.

IMPORTANT NOTICE

Extract from Bye-Laws made by the Commissioners of Health for the Parish of St. Michael for the City

2. The occupiers of all houses, stores, warehouses, or other premises within the limits of the city shall daily have swept and

cleaned the yards and enclosures thereof, the streets, pavements and gutters in front of and around the same, as far as the centre of the streets, some time before the hour of eight every morning ; and shall collect the sweepings and rubbish, with other refuse matter on their premises, in a box or some other receptacle, to be placed ready to hand on the premises for removal by the scavengers' carts. And where such premises are not occupied, it shall be the duty of the owners to have the streets, pavements and gutters daily swept and cleansed, and the rubbish removed or deposited as aforesaid for removal by the carts.

Extract from Bye-Laws for Suburbs of Bridgetown

No. 4. The owners or occupiers of all houses or other premises throughout the city and suburbs are required at all times to keep such premises in every respect clean and free from offensive matter and rubbish of every kind ; and the occupiers or owners of all houses, stores, or other premises within the *suburbs* shall have swept and cleaned the yards and enclosures thereof, and gutters in front of, and around, the said premises.

Extract from the General Board of Health Rules, 22nd February, 1909, confirmed by the Governor in Executive Committee on February 26, and proclaimed in the Official Gazette on March 1, 1909

2. The occupier or owner of any premises shall keep such premises free of stagnant water, liable to breed mosquitos, and the presence of mosquito larvæ, in any collection of water, wherever situated, shall be sufficient evidence that such water is stagnant. All tanks, fountains, pools, ponds, or excavations made for any purpose whatever, in public or private property, which may contain water, shall be kept stocked with mosquito-destroying fish, or shall be kept covered with a film of petroleum oil.

3. The occupier or owner of any premises shall keep his premises free of articles (bottles whole or broken, old tins, boxes, conch shells, etc.) which may retain water and so become the breeding place of mosquitos.

4. All cess-pits which retain water shall be disinfected or oiled except they be efficiently covered and trapped.

5. All gutters and down-pipes shall be maintained in good repair and free of obstruction so as to prevent the accumulation of water therein and to allow the ready passage of water from the roofs of houses.

6. All Inspectors of Health shall have authority to enter any

premises at any time between the hours of 7 a.m. to 6 p.m. for the purpose of seeing that these Regulations are carried out, and may pour oil or cause oil to be poured on the surface of water contained in any receptacle in or on such premises.

Penalty for infringement of Bye-Laws of the Commissioners of Health, a sum not exceeding £5.

Penalty for infringement of Rules of the General Board of Health, a sum not exceeding £10, to be recovered before a Police Magistrate.

By order,
S. E. BREWSTER,
Inspector of Health, No. 2 District.

THE BAHAMAS, NASSAU

Measures were first taken in 1905 by the Board of Health against mosquito-borne diseases. In 1906 the authorities circulated my pamphlet upon the prevention of Yellow Fever and imported wire-gauze for distribution. In 1907 the following useful antilarval regulations were drawn up and circularised, and quinine was distributed at cost price and free of cost to the poor.

BOARD OF HEALTH ACT, 1872

RULES AND REGULATIONS, OCTOBER 1907

1. The owner or person in control of any cistern, vat, tank, barrel, bucket, or other vessel used for the storage of water shall within such time as may be specified by notice protect the same from mosquitos in the following manner, that is to say:

   i. Cisterns, tanks, vats, and barrels shall be provided with covers of wood or metal, and all openings other than the delivery exit shall be screened with netting.

   ii. Buckets and similar or other retainers shall be protected in the same way as cisterns, or in some other manner approved by the Board.

   iii. Owners and occupiers of premises on which there is any water in wells, ponds, pools or basins, or in depressions or excavations made for any purpose, or which by any means have occurred, and in which mosquitos can breed, shall within such time as may be specified by notice protect the same from mosquitos in the following manner, that is to say—

   (1) Stock them with mosquito-destroying fish ;

(2) Or cover them with protective netting;

(3) Or drain them off at least once a week;

(4) Or cover them with oil at least once every week : or fill them up.

(5) Or (in case of wells) provide them with a pump and mosquito-proof cover to the satisfaction of the Board.

3. All empty and open tins shall be kept in such a position as to prevent mosquitos breeding in them, and all odd receptacles, such as jars, broken crockery, condensed milk tins and other rubbish which form receptacles for water shall be removed and buried. All doreys, pit-pans and boats, in use or discarded, must be kept free of fresh water.

PENALTIES

4. Any person committing a breach of any of these Rules and Regulations shall be liable on summary conviction to a penalty of £2, and on a second conviction to a penalty not exceeding £5 or to imprisonment with or without hard labour not exceeding 30 days.

NOTICE

5. " Notice " shall mean a written notice addressed by a person authorised in that behalf by the Board to the occupier or the owner of any premises, or water receptacle, and every such notice shall be deemed to have been duly served by delivering the same or a duplicate thereof to some person on the premises, or if there is no person on the premises who can be so served, by fixing the same on some conspicuous part of the premises, or in the case of a water receptacle as aforesaid by fixing the same on the water receptacle in respect of which such notice is issued.

J. BENSON ALBURY, M.D.,
Chairman of Board of Health.

MAURITIUS. PROPOSED ANTILARVAL AND DRAINAGE MEASURES, 1908

ORDINANCE NO. · OF 1908

1. In this Ordinance " owner," " occupier," " premises," "sanitary authority" shall have the same meaning as in Ordinance No. 32 of 1894-5.

2. The following paragraph is added to Article 29 of Ordinance 32 of 1894-5.

All collections of water, sewage, rubbish, refuse, ordure, or other fluid or solid substances, and all other conditions which permit, or facilitate, or are likely to permit or facilitate, the breeding or multiplication of animal or vegetable parasites of men or domestic animals, or of insects or other agents which are known to carry such parasites, or which may otherwise cause or facilitate the infection of men or domestic animals by such parasites.

3. (a) Notwithstanding the above provisions or any of the provisions of Ordinances No. 32 of 1894-5, 21 of 1903, 12 of 1889, 31 and 32 of 1895—

It shall be lawful for any Sanitary Authority or any person deputed by him in writing to take immediate steps to destroy mosquito larvæ on any premises where they may be found, and to take such action as may be necessary to render any pools or accumulations of water unfit to be breeding places for mosquitos.

(b) The persons so deputed shall have a right to enter any premises, dwelling-houses excepted, between the hours of six in the morning and six in the afternoon.

(c) When such pools or accumulations of water lie on premises under the charge of a public body or corporation they shall not be dealt with as above provided, unless due warning has been given in writing to such public body or corporation, and no action has within reasonable delay, not to be less than 24 hours, been taken by them. In such cases the expenditure incurred shall be borne by such public body or corporation.

(d) Any owner or occupier who shall object to pools and collections of water on his premises being dealt with as above provided shall within 24 hours submit his reasons to the Sanitary Authority, who, after inquiry, shall order such action to be taken as he shall consider necessary to meet the provisions of this Ordinance. Should the objections be rejected the measures originally ordered shall be carried out at the expense of the said owner or occupier.

4. It shall not be lawful for any owner or occupier to allow mosquitos to breed on his premises or to allow the presence on such premises of any receptacles in which water is kept or may collect unless such receptacles are properly protected from access of mosquitos, or unless the water they may contain is treated in such a way as to prevent the breeding therein of mosquitos, nor shall such owner or occupier allow on his premises any conditions which may, in any way, be favourable to the breeding of mosquitos.

5. Trees on all premises shall be at all times kept freely lopped to the satisfaction of the Sanitary Authority by the owner

or occupier, and no trees shall be allowed to grow within ten feet from any dwelling-house. The Sanitary Authority may, in writing, direct the said owner or occupier to carry out the above provision within a reasonable delay, not to be less than 48 hours, and, in case of non-compliance, the trees shall be lopped or cut down at the expense of the owner or occupier.[1]

6. It shall be lawful for the Director of the Health Department to make such regulations as may be necessary to carry out the provisions of this Ordinance.

7. It shall be lawful for the Director of the Health Department, in any case when the owner or occupier of any premises is liable for the expense of any measures carried out on his premises, to relieve such owner or occupier from the said expense, if, after inquiry, the Director is satisfied that such owner or occupier is not in a position to incur such expense. In such cases the expenditure shall be borne by Government.

8. Any person acting in breach of Articles 4 and 5, or of the regulations made under Article 6, shall be liable to a fine not exceeding Rs. 100.

9. Expenses incurred by the Sanitary Authority under paragraphs (c) and (d) of Article 3, and under Article 5, shall be dealt with in the manner provided by Articles 52 and 53 of Ordinance No. 32 of 1894–5.

10. This Ordinance may be cited as the Malaria Prevention Ordinance.

WEST AFRICA

In the year 1905 clauses were inserted by Dr. Prout, C.M.G., in the Public Health Ordinance of Sierra Leone dealing with mosquito larvæ, and it was made a nuisance under this Ordinance (1905) to have any collection of water in any well, pool, channel, barrel, tub, bucket or any other vessel, and found by the Sanitary Authority to contain *mosquito larvæ.*

Under clause 4, paragraph (d) it states:

When mosquito larvæ are found in any collection of water, or in any well or pool, channel, barrel, tub, bucket, or in any other vessel, the Sanitary Authority may themselves abate the same, and may do what is necessary to prevent the recurrence thereof.

[1] Some specific provision ought to be made to enable the Sanitary Authority to fill up with concrete, or otherwise to treat, holes and hollows in trees which breed, or are likely to breed, mosquitos ; and also to compel owners to cut insanitary undergrowth (see particularly addendum 3).

R. Ross.

PENALTIES

Where a notice has been served on a person under this section (4)—

Where mosquito larvæ are found in any collection of water or in any well or pool, channel, barrel, tub, bucket, or any other vessel, within ten days from the service of such notice on any such person in respect of any such collection of water, well, pool, channel, barrel, tub, bucket or other vessel, he shall be liable to a fine not exceeding ten pounds for each offence, whether any such nuisance order as in this Ordinance mentioned is or is not made upon him.

Under Section 31 dealing with provisions as to water, it is stated :

Every person who shall keep an any premises any collection of water in any well, barrel, tub, bucket or other vessel intended for the storage of water without providing them with covers so constructed as to prevent the ingress of mosquitos into the same, shall be liable to a fine not exceeding twenty shillings. If a person shall fail to comply with the provisions of this section, he shall, after notice received from the Sanitary Authority to comply therewith, be liable to a further fine not exceeding seventy shillings a day during his default.

THE ANTIPLAGUE CAMPAIGN IN SAN FRANCISCO

There has just been issued an account of the eradication of plague in San Francisco. It is a very excellent and stimulating account of what has been accomplished, and it should serve to stimulate this country to wake up to do likewise for India.

As was the case during the 1905 yellow fever outbreak, so in San Francisco one of the first steps was the organisation of a Citizens' Health Committee to combat the plague which had burst out again in 1909. This committee organised in all the useful directions, and at the end of six weeks reported as follows :

42,460 premises inspected,
334 premises disinfected,
171 dangerous houses destroyed,
54 buildings condemned,
17,564 nuisances abated,
56,994 rats trapped or poisoned.

The committee had enlisted the sympathy of the entire population. One hundred meetings had taken place ; a vast quantity of literature had been distributed ; numerous improvement clubs had been organised throughout the city. With regard to the support given by the clergy, the Report states :

Rat destruction, cleanliness and sanitary doctrine in general were preached in the churches and sabbath schools for several months. A general meeting of the clergy of all denominations was held in the Chamber of Commerce to advance the sanitary crusade.

The Report further remarks .

Before San Francisco could get rid of plague it had to go to school and study zoology, bacteriology and fleas. The whole community had to learn about plague as a disease and an epidemic—*that plague was a rat disease.*

Again, the Report adds :

Fleas shun the sunlight and the air. They deposit their eggs in rat-nests and the rats hatch them out with the warmth of their bodies and then give the young fleas free transportation wherever they go. Sulphur fumes will kill them, so that fumigation has been found effective.

Ordinances were passed by the Mayor and Council of San Francisco :

(*a*) Dealing with the collecting of garbage.
(*b*) The suitable construction of all stables, which were further sources of rat breeding.
(*c*) The proper flooring of markets and yards and basements.
(*d*) The keeping of animals and fowls.
(*e*) The suppression of insanitary buildings and many other matters.

The Report makes some ugly comparisons between what has been accomplished in San Francisco with what is occurring in India to-day. It says in 1896 the plague reached Bombay and is still there. It has spread all over India, and in the face of modern medical skill it has claimed over five and a quarter million victims. In 1904, the year the first epidemic was suppressed in San Francisco, it killed over a million people in the Indian Empire, destroying in a single week over 76,000 lives—a number equal to the British Army in India !

LIST OF COMMISSIONS AND EXPEDITIONS SENT TO THE TROPICS TO STUDY TROPICAL DISEASES

ROYAL SOCIETY

INVESTIGATIONS INTO TROPICAL DISEASES CARRIED OUT UNDER THE DIRECTION OF COMMITTEES OF THE ROYAL SOCIETY

TSETSE FLY.—No expedition sent out, but investigations carried on in Natal by Surgeon-Major (now Colonel Sir David) Bruce more or less independently of the Committee, and by Dr. W. H. F. Blandford, Dr. Kanthack, and Dr. H. E. Durham in London under the direction of the Committee, in 1896 and 1897.

MALARIA AND BLACKWATER FEVER.—Dr. C. W. Daniels, Dr. J. W. W. Stephens, and S. R. Christophers, M.B., sent to British Central Africa in 1898. Daniels also to East Africa and Stephens and Christophers to West Coast. Stephens and Christophers sent to India in 1901 to carry out researches on Blackwater and Malaria. returned to England in 1902 ; work on Malaria continued by Captain James, I.M.S.

SLEEPING SICKNESS.—Dr. G. C. Low, Dr. C. Christy, Dr. A. Castellani, sent to Uganda in June 1902. In 1903, Colonel Bruce and Dr. Nabarro joined the Commission. In 1904-5 the work of the Commission was conducted by Captain Grieg and Lieutenant Gray, R.A.M.C. In 1908 Colonel Sir David Bruce again left for Uganda in September, accompanied by Captains A. E. Hammerton and H. R. Bateman, R.A.M.C. This Commission is still in Uganda.

MEDITERRANEAN FEVER.—The first Commission was sent out in 1904, and consisted of Major Horrocks, R.A.M.C., Staff Surgeon Shaw, R.N., and Dr. Zammet, under Colonel Bruce, R.A.M.C. In 1905 the Commission consisted of Staff Surgeon Shaw, R.N., Dr. Kennedy, R.A.M.C., Major Horrocks, R.A.M.C., and Lieut.-Colonel Davies, R.A.M.C., under Colonel Bruce. In 1906, the members of the Commission under Colonel Bruce were Major McCulloch, R.A.M.C., Major Weir, R.A.M.C., and Major McNaught, R.A.M.C., Staff Surgeon Clayton, and Dr. Eyre.

The brilliant work of these Commissions is published in a series of Reports issued by the Royal Society.

LIVERPOOL SCHOOL OF TROPICAL MEDICINE

The following is a complete list of the Expeditions sent out to the Tropics from the commencement of the School to the end of 1908 :—

THE FIRST (MALARIAL) EXPEDITION : Major Ronald Ross, C.B., F.R.S., Dr. H. E. Annett, Mr. E. E. Austen (of the British Museum), and Dr. Van Neck (of Belgium), despatched to Sierra Leone in the summer of 1899.

THE SECOND (MALARIAL) EXPEDITION : Dr. R. Fielding Ould, despatched to the Gold Coast and Lagos in the winter of 1899.

THE THIRD (MALARIAL) EXPEDITION : Dr. H. E. Annett, Dr. J. Dutton, and Dr. Elliot, despatched to Northern and Southern Nigeria in the spring of 1900.

THE FOURTH (YELLOW FEVER) EXPEDITION : Dr. H. E. Durham and the late Dr. Walter Myers, despatched to Cuba, and to Pará, Brazil, in the summer of 1900.

THE FIFTH (SANITATION) EXPEDITION : Major Ronald Ross, C.B., F.R.S., and Dr. Logan Taylor, despatched to Sierra Leone in the early summer of 1901.

THE SIXTH (TRYPANOSOMIASIS) EXPEDITION : Dr. J. E. Dutton, despatched to the Gambia in the autumn of 1901.

THE SEVENTH (MALARIAL) EXPEDITION : Dr. C. Balfour Stewart, despatched to the Gold Coast in November 1901.

THE EIGHTH (SANITATION) EXPEDITION : Major Ross, despatched to Sierra Leone on February 22, 1902.

THE NINTH (MALARIAL) EXPEDITION : Major Ross accompanied by Sir William MacGregor, K.C.M.G., the Governor of Lagos, despatched to Ismailia, September 11, 1902.

THE TENTH (TRYPANOSOMIASIS) EXPEDITION : Dr. J. E. Dutton and Dr. J. L. Todd, despatched to the Gambia and French Senegal on September 21, 1902. This Expedition received great assistance from M. Roume, Governor-General of French West Africa, and all the French officials with whom they came in contact. Two valuable Reports in connection with the Expedition have been issued by the School.

THE ELEVENTH (SANITATION) EXPEDITION : Dr. M. Logan Taylor, despatched to the Gold Coast from Sierra Leone on October 11, 1902. This Expedition was sent to the Gold Coast in consequence of unsatisfactory rumours as to the health of that district. The services of Dr. Taylor were utilised by the Governor of the Colony, and his recommendations for improving the sanitary conditions of Cape Coast Castle carried out with most successful results.

THE TWELFTH (TRYPANOSOMIASIS) EXPEDITION : Dr. J. E. Dutton, Dr. J. L. Todd, and Dr. C. Christy, despatched to the Congo Free State on September 23, 1903. This Expedition gives promise of being the most important Expedition sent out by the School since the Expedition in 1899, which discovered the presence of the Anopheles Mosquito in West Africa. It was sent out as a result of representations made to the School by H.M. the King of the Belgians, who made the Expedition possible by granting a handsome donation towards its expenses.

THE THIRTEENTH EXPEDITION : Professor Rubert Boyce, M.B., F.R.S., Dr. Arthur Evans, M.R.C.S., and Dr. Herbert H. Clarke, M.A., B.C. (Cantab.), were despatched to Bathurst, Conakry and Freetown on November 14, 1904, to report on the Sanitation and Antimalarial Measures in practice at the towns visited. The members of the Expedition have drawn up a valuable Report, which has been issued by the School.

THE FOURTEENTH EXPEDITION : Lieut.-Col. G. M. Giles, M.B., F.R.S., Indian Medical Service (Rtd.), and Dr. R. Ernest McConnell, M.D. (Canada), despatched to the Gold Coast on December 31, 1904. Unfortunately, Col. Giles had to return to England on February 8, 1905, through illness. Dr. McConnell remained for several months on the Coast to carry on the work of the Expedition.

The Thirteenth and Fourteenth Expeditions were sent to West Africa in appreciation of Sir William MacGregor's great services to health and sanitation in West Africa.

THE FIFTEENTH (YELLOW FEVER) EXPEDITION : Dr. H. Wolferstan Thomas and Dr. Anton Breinl, despatched to the Amazon in April 1905. Both members of the Expedition contracted yellow fever and Dr. Breinl had to be invalided home. Dr. Thomas is still carrying on the work of the Expedition.

THE SIXTEENTH (YELLOW FEVER) EXPEDITION : Professor Boyce, F.R.S., despatched to New Orleans in August 1905 to observe the work of the United States Medical Authorities in dealing with the outbreak of yellow fever there. Professor Boyce subsequently visited British Honduras at the special request of the Colonial Office, to make a report on the conditions existing in that Colony with reference to a recent outbreak of Yellow Fever.

THE SEVENTEENTH (MALARIAL) EXPEDITION: Professor Ross, C.B., despatched to Lake Copias, in Greece, on May 20, 1906, at the request of the Lake Copias Company.

THE EIGHTEENTH (SLEEPING SICKNESS) EXPEDITION : Dr. Allan Kinghorn, M.B , and Mr. R. E. Montgomery, M.R.C.V.S.,despatched to Rhodesia and British Central Africa on May 5, 1907.

THE NINETEENTH (BLACKWATER FEVER) EXPEDITION : Dr. J. O. Wakelin Barratt, M.D., D.Sc. (Lond.), and Dr. W. Yorke, M.D., despatched to Nyassaland on August 14, 1907.

THE TWENTIETH EXPEDITION : Professor Ronald Ross, C.B., despatched to Mauritius on October 28, 1907.

THE TWENTY-FIRST EXPEDITION . R. Newstead, M.Sc., A.L.S., F.E.S., Dr. W. T. Prout, M.B., C.M.G., and Dr. Alan Hanley, M.D., C.M.G., despatched to Jamaica on November 14, 1908.

EXPEDITIONS ORGANISED BY THE LONDON SCHOOL OF TROPICAL MEDICINE

1900. MALARIA.—Drs. Sambon and Low practically demonstrated that in the Roman Campagna, Malaria could not be acquired without the mosquito.

1902. FILARIASIS.—Dr. Low went to the West Indies to study Filariasis and the relationship of Mosquitos to disease.

1902. SLEEPING SICKNESS.—Drs. Low and Castellani members of the Royal Society's Commission in Uganda.

1902. BERI-BERI. Dr. Durham went to Christmas Island to investigate this disease and afterwards proceeded to Singapore and the Malay States.

1905. Dr. Leiper : investigations upon the Guinea Worm, West Africa.

1907. Dr. Wenyon: investigations in Egypt and the Soudan.

1908. Professor Simpson : Plague investigations in West Africa for Colonial Office.

INDEX

261

Printed by Hazell, Watson & Viney, Ld., London and Aylesbury.

(Clonorchis - Sinensis)
Liver fluke - (China)
very prevalent in Calif. in
Can cerns conditions,
(Dr. alfred c.Read, 4V. of Calif,) the U
(anotter ch _ _ _ _ _ Gen

U

Printed in Great Britain
by Amazon